"This is my new favorite book about goals! Jon Acuff has done it again!"

Mel Robbins, podcaster and *New York Times* bestselling author of *The High 5 Habit*

"Wow! This is one of those rare books that will make you take action and see serious results immediately. Really."

Patrick Lencioni, bestselling author of *The Five Dysfunctions of a Team* and *The Six Types of Working Genius*

"The best book about goals I've ever read! Jon Acuff and *All It Takes Is a Goal* will help you achieve your greatest potential!"

Jon Gordon, twelve-time bestselling author of *The Power of Positive Leadership*

"I have often said that the richest place on earth is the cemetery because so many people die with unrealized potential still in them. Maybe they were surrounded by people who didn't believe in them, or maybe they didn't even know they were capable of more. But in *All It Takes Is a Goal*, Jon Acuff brilliantly provides the road map to activating the potential within us. This book should be required reading for everyone with breath in their lungs."

Nona Jones, speaker, technology executive, and author of *Killing Comparison*

"If you know what it feels like to be stuck in a car, then you'll appreciate finding someone with a big truck to give you a tug in the right direction. My friend Jon has written another terrific book, and his is a voice I have trusted in my life for years. In these pages he won't push you around, and he will gently

tap you on the shoulder, remind you of your goals, and pull you in the delightful direction you were headed before you became stuck, distracted, discouraged, or off course."

Bob Goff, author of the *New York Times* bestsellers *Love Does*, *Everybody Always*, *Dream Big*, and *Undistracted*

"Captivating, relatable, and humorous from the first page until the last, Jon opens up the door to his personal experiences with an honesty that drives readers to accurately reflect on our own lives. More than that, he walks us down an entertaining and insightful path toward a better life in a step-by-step fashion, guaranteed to work no matter what our aspirations are."

Ginny Yurich, founder of 1000 Hours Outside

"This book will help you reach your goals, but it will do more than that. It will help you take responsibility for your life. If you're looking for the inspiration and instruction you need to shape your own world, you're holding it in your hands."

Donald Miller, CEO of Business Made Simple

"MASTERFUL! This is Jon Acuff's best work. Goals are so elusive and abstract, yet Jon does a marvelous job taking the complicated and making it simple and actionable. I fully believe this book is the difference between waking up ten years from now in a pool of regret OR waking up having accomplished your goals and living the life you have always wanted to live. It is THAT powerful!"

David Nurse, bestselling author, Top 50 Keynote Speaker, and NBA Optimization Coach to over 150 NBA stars

"Twelve years ago, I read a draft of Jon Acuff's first business book. I immediately emailed him and said, 'Whatever other plans you have, reconsider them and start writing full-time. You're wasting yourself, baby!' I'm glad he took that advice to heart. If you've ever wondered if you're capable of more, consider this book the resounding 'Yes!' you've been waiting for all your life."

Steven Pressfield, *New York Times* bestselling author of *The War of Art*

"Jon has done it again: a fresh, funny, and inspiring work that will help take your results to the next level! Prepare to unlock your potential and 10X your life."

Greg McKeown, podcaster and *New York Times* bestselling author of *Essentialism* and *Effortless*

"Jon has the rare and wonderful gift of making you see perennial obstacles with fresh eyes. A cut above the 'usual' advice on goal setting, Jon's fresh, hyperpractical, and humorous approach will make you think thoughts you've never had before and do things you've never done before. This is the breakthrough you've been looking for."

Carey Nieuwhof, podcaster, bestselling author of *At Your Best*, and founder of The Art of Leadership Academy

ALL IT TAKES IS A GOAL

ALL IT TAKES IS A GOAL

The 3-Step Plan to Ditch Regret and Tap Into Your Massive Potential

JON ACUFF

BakerBooks

a division of Baker Publishing Group
Grand Rapids, Michigan

© 2023 by Jon Acuff

Published by Baker Books
a division of Baker Publishing Group
Grand Rapids, Michigan
www.bakerbooks.com

Printed in the United States of America

Library of Congress Cataloging-in-Publication Data
Names: Acuff, Jon, author.
Title: All it takes is a goal : the 3-step plan to ditch regret and tap into your massive
    potential / Jon Acuff.
Description: Grand Rapids, Micigan : Baker Books, a division of Baker Publishing
    Group, [2023] | Includes bibliographical references.
Identifiers: LCCN 2023002260 | ISBN 9781540900814 (cloth) | ISBN 9781540903952
    (paperback) | ISBN 9781493443185 (ebook)
Subjects: LCSH: Goal (Psychology) | Success—Psychological aspects.
Classification: LCC BF505.G6 A33 2023 | DDC 153.8/5—dc23/eng/20230321
LC record available at https://lccn.loc.gov/2023002260

Some names and identifying details have been changed to protect the privacy of individuals.

Published in association with Yates & Yates, www.yates2.com.

Baker Publishing Group publications use paper produced from sustainable forestry practices and post-consumer waste whenever possible.

Interior design by William Overbeeke.

23 24 25 26 27 28 29   7 6 5 4 3 2 1

For Mrs. Harris,
my third grade teacher
in Ipswich, Massachusetts,
who taught me that writing was easy
if you make it a goal.

CONTENTS

Introduction: Frustrated and Curious about Potential   13

THE LIST

1. Go Back to the Future   21

2. Build Your Best Moments List   35

3. Conquer the Future by Categorizing the Past   44

4. Trick the Hardest Person to Change   57

THE ZONES

5. Navigate the Three Performance Zones   75

6. Pick the Big Game You Want to Win   84

7. Escape the Comfort Zone with an Easy Goal   97

8. Skip the Chaos Zone with a Middle Goal   107

9. Plan a Calendar Heist   120

THE FUEL

10. Find Your Favorite Fuel   141

11. Achieve the Best Kind of Accomplishment   150

12. Get Crafty without Any Glitter   159

13. Find Your People, Find Your Potential   168

14. Own More Stories and Fewer Objects   180

THE PROMISE

15. Guarantee Your Success   193

16. Turn Fears into Goals and Watch Them Fall   213

17. Create a Scorecard to Know That You're Winning   228

Conclusion: Go Back Down the Goal Ladder   249

Acknowledgments   257

Notes   259

INTRODUCTION

Frustrated and Curious about Potential

I didn't think about living up to my full potential until I was forty-five years old. What can I say? I'm a late bloomer.

When I finally did, I got frustrated and curious.

The frustration started when I took a college tour with my oldest daughter one crisp October day. I wasn't expecting to feel anything but excitement for her in that moment, but a rogue wave of disappointment knocked me over midway through the visit.

My wife and I were standing next to each other, overlooking the quad at Samford University in Birmingham, Alabama, but we were having completely opposite experiences.

She was remembering our shared alma mater with fondness. Her wistful eyes were sweeping the campus, and she was having a hard time deciding which of the hundreds of memories was her favorite. "Wasn't college just the best?" she asked me, squeezing my arm for emphasis.

"What? No. It was a mess," I said, scanning the same exact acres she was but instead seeing my collegiate train wreck.

I had arrived in Alabama from my hometown of Hudson, Massachusetts, with a *Good Will Hunting* level of sarcasm that quickly got me rejected from every fraternity on campus. I was put on social suspension for a year after a disastrous Halloween prank, and I ended up working at the shaved ice stand outside our local Walmart. This wasn't inside the Walmart—this was an unaffiliated street cart that a man named Kevin just rolled onto the sidewalk near the entrance. Is that what you did during your first semester of college? Unlocked "shaved ice guy" level at Walmart?

I'd like to say I turned things around after my freshman year, but then we'd have to overlook my foray into rave culture. Yes, I wore reflective clothing and danced in warehouses with glowsticks at 3:00 a.m. during my senior year. I guess I wanted to put a neon cap on my college career, an electronic bow on what might have been.

Standing there twenty-five years later, I was so frustrated that I had wasted all the potential of college. A university campus practically crackles with possibility. The opportunity to be something, do something, become something is everywhere you look. My oldest daughter was about to make the most of it. My wife had already made the most of it. But I hadn't. How could I have missed it?

On the drive back home to Nashville and in the weeks ahead, that question weighed heavy on me. In the past, that sense of regret would've turned into bitterness and resignation. Have you ever felt that way after bumping into an opportunity you missed or a chance you blew? That's my normal response, but this time was different. I'd spent the previous two years researching and writing about the power of mindset for a book I published called *Soundtracks*. I knew that one of the best things you can do with a negative soundtrack (my phrase for a repetitive thought) is ask, "Is this helpful?" Bitterness never is, so instead I decided to see if I could flip my frustration into curiosity.

Maybe it was my age. Your forties hit different. They make you more introspective about where you've been and where you're headed. My wife and I were also two years away from being empty nesters. There were significant changes on the horizon, and I started to ask the questions about my life that smarter people ask in their twenties and thirties.

I didn't live up to my potential in college. That's true and I can't change it, but I started to wonder if I could change something even better—my future. Could I change this week? Could I change this month or even the whole year? College was only four years long. I still had decades of life ahead of me.

I was late to my thirties, so I wanted to be early to my fifties. I didn't make the most of my twenties and ended up in my thirties without a real plan or foundation for my life. I wasn't about to let that same thing happen again for my fifties, sixties, and beyond.

I didn't know if living up to my full potential was possible, but I had a sneaking suspicion that I was capable of more, and I wanted to know what I could do about that.

Turns out I'm not the only one who feels that way.

Tapping Into Our Potential

When I got curious about tapping into my full potential, I did what I always do when I get curious: I commissioned a research study with Dr. Mike Peasley, a professor at Middle

Tennessee State University. He and I asked more than three thousand people if they felt they were living up to their full potential.

Only 4 percent of them said yes.

That's a surprisingly low statistic, but it's not the one that stood out to me the most.

According to our study, 50 percent of people feel that 50 percent of their full potential is untapped. That means half of us are walking around with half-lives. No wonder Twitter is so grumpy.

Imagine if every Christmas you only opened up half your gifts. You could see the rest—a whole pile of them in the corner of the room—but you never got to open them. The crazy thing is that no one was stopping you. There might even be friends and family members encouraging you to open them all, but for some reason they just felt out of reach.

According to our study, 50 percent of people feel that 50 percent of their full potential is untapped.

Would that make for a happy Christmas, a happy house, a happy job, a happy anything?

It wouldn't, but what if it didn't have to be that way?

What if you could have a fulfilling career?

What if you could enjoy a thriving marriage and strong friendships?

What if you could be in the greatest shape of your life?

What if you could write that book, start that business, declutter that garage, and pay to fly your immigrant parents first-class back to the Netherlands so they could finally see the tulip festival?

What if each day felt like a gift and each year progressively got better?

If you're in your twenties, what if that could be your favorite decade, followed by your thirties, which was even more fun, and then your forties, which somehow managed to top those two?

That would be the best.

Let's Keep This Simple

What if I could turn potential into a goal? What if all it takes is a goal? That would certainly simplify an otherwise confusing challenge.

You can't take action on an idea you can't even define, and *potential* is such a fuzzy word. It's like trying to win a race without a finish line. You don't know if you're headed in the right direction, you can't tell if you're making any progress, and you tend to get frustrated by the whole process.

That's what I sensed people were struggling with when I asked them to define *potential.* Their answers were all over the map:

A feeling of purpose

Joy

No regrets

Freedom to do what I choose

Maximum effectiveness

Those seemed like aspects of potential, but they didn't add a lot of actionable clarity to the conversation. Feelings are an important light to monitor on the dashboard of your life, but they can also be inconsistent and flighty.

What about joy? How do you measure that? Is there some sort of scale or color system? "I'm deep orange today, which is the amount of joy I can expect on a Tuesday. I hope I'm magenta by Friday."

No regrets? Daniel Pink's book *The Power of Regret* proved that while "No regrets" is a popular tattoo, it's also an impossible thing to achieve. The average person makes up to 35,000 decisions a day.[1] Have you ever gone 35,000 for 35,000 on a Monday? Me neither. Even the most calculated, careful life ends up with some regrets.

Maximum effectiveness? That sounds like a robot. "I HAVE ACHIEVED MAXIMUM EFFECTIVENESS BUT REQUIRE SUSTENANCE."

What if life was simpler than that though?

The more I thought about it, the more I kept coming back to one critical question: What if all it takes is a goal?

Could I trigger a host of easy goals that would cascade into big accomplishments by turning this thing I suddenly cared about—my potential—into a goal?

Could I use that idea to become part of the 4 percent who say, "Yes! I am living up to my full potential!"

I only had the tiniest sliver of belief at first, but that was all I needed to start.

Equipped with that one idea, I began to seriously explore the concept of potential. Everything was great for about fourteen seconds, until I ran into the same wall you've hit before.

THE LIST

1

Go Back to the Future

"What do you want to be when you grow up?" That question paralyzes me.

I wish it didn't. I wish dreaming about the future was something I was better at. I wish I didn't freeze up when people ask, "What's your big, hairy, audacious goal?" but I do.

This is my seventh self-help book, so you'd think I'd be better at imagining the future, but I'm not. When I initially started working on my potential, I ran into the same obstacle I'd bumped into a thousand times before—the Vision Wall.

The Vision Wall is the gateway that stands between you and your potential. It has only one rule: in order to fulfill your potential you must first create a detailed, compelling, long-reaching vision for your life. I didn't invent this wall; nearly every life-planning book ever written has added to it brick by brick.

The most famous example is from Stephen Covey's *The 7 Habits of Highly Effective People*. Habit number 2 is "Begin with the end in mind." After millions of copies sold and millions of misinterpretations were shared, that idea has mutated to "If you don't know the end, you can't begin." Covey didn't write that, but that's what the Vision Wall tells you he meant.

More recently, the Vision Wall turned Simon Sinek's popular *Start with Why* into "Don't try until you know why."

The Vision Wall is the gateway that stands between you and your potential.

This brilliant book doesn't actually set up the concept that way, but the Vision Wall doesn't fight fair. What started out as an insightful directive meant to help companies like Apple figure out their ethos became a mythical key individuals needed to acquire before tapping into their potential. I once watched a friend spend six months trying to figure out his why with books, coaches, and personality tests. He was convinced that as soon as he knew that, everything else would fall into place.

Who can blame him? The Vision Wall tells you, "No why? No try."

Entrepreneurs hit the Vision Wall when experts tell them they must know their microniche before starting a business. You can't be a florist; that's too broad. You should decide to focus on selling Gold of Kinabalu orchids from Malaysia to redheaded interior designers from San Diego who are named Alexis. It took me twenty-five years of full-time professional writing to hone in on my niche and target audience, but you should know yours before you start.

Living out of your full potential is easy then. All you have to do is predict the end, discover your why, and correctly identify your microniche with laserlike precision. Then you can begin.

Fake Deaths, Fake Cars, and Real Problems

In order to scale the Vision Wall, we often try gimmicks like imagining we're dying as a backdoor to motivation. If you only had six months to live, what would you put on your bucket list? These sorts of exercises, which I've written about before and tried in my own life, immediately fall apart in the real world. If I were dying, I wouldn't bother to pay my taxes, file invoices with clients, be nice to difficult neighbors, fold laundry, or a million other annoying things a full life requires. I'd be too busy skydiving, Rocky Mountain climbing, watching an eagle as it was flying, and the sundry other items in Tim McGraw's appropriately named song "Live Like You Were Dying."

Although positive post-traumatic growth has been shown to occur for people who survive illness and loss, I haven't met a single person who had a sustained life change after rallying around an imaginary health scare. Momentary motivation? Sure. Long-term fulfillment? Nope.

You haven't met that person either. "What really changed my life? An imaginary car crash off an imaginary bridge into an imaginary river. I swore when I finally swam to shore that I was going to imagine being a new person!"

I didn't know my end, and I didn't know my why. If anything, I felt completely divorced from my desire. We saw each other on holidays and occasional vacations, but for the most part desire felt like a total stranger to me. "To thine own self be true" is helpful if you know who you are, but I didn't, which is why for years I thought I was a Jeep guy.

In my thirties I dreamed about one day owning a Jeep Wrangler. I built them online constantly. I oohed and aahed every time I saw one. I imagined a future where I required a snorkel on the side of my rig because I was regularly fording creeks and whatnot. Shovel attached to the hood? Need it. Spare gas can on the back for particularly long off-road expeditions? Add it. Tiny three-rung ladder offering two feet of additional visibility? Better throw that on there, too, because I plan to constantly be on that roof. I talked to Jeep owners and promised that I'd start doing the Jeep wave when we passed each other on the road as soon as I owned one.

After hearing me talk about Jeeps for a decade, my wife Jenny finally had enough. When we sat down to talk about buying a new car, she surprised me and said, "I don't think you'd even like a Jeep."

I was flabbergasted. I should've just told her, "It's a Jeep thing, you wouldn't understand," but we've been to a lot of marriage counseling, so instead I practiced reflective listening.

"When you say, 'You wouldn't like a Jeep,' what do you mean?" I asked her.

"You're not an outdoors guy. You hate getting dirty, you mildly tolerate camping because I love it, and you're furious when you step on a melted ice cube in the kitchen and get your sock wet," she said.

"Yeah, because it's like carrying around a puddle with you all day on your foot. But I've always been a Jeep guy. If I'm not a Jeep guy, what am I supposed to do with this 'Salt Life' sticker?"

"I don't know about that, but I think you're a hot hatch guy."

I didn't even know what that phrase meant, but a week later we were test driving a little red Volkswagen GTI hatchback. A week and ten minutes later, I was in love. A month later I was trying to Tokyo drift my way into parking spots because my go-kart-like car was so fun to drive.

That's how disconnected I was from what I really like. And that was just the car I drive. Imagine how confused I was about my vision for the future. One is a vehicle; the other is what I want to do with the rest of my life.

If you have to know your future to change your present, I was screwed. I couldn't even envision the type of car I'd like.

There had to be another way.

The Rearview Mirror

I had decades of evidence that the popular approach to potential didn't work for me, and I bet it doesn't work for you either. That's because when you sit down and try to plot out the future, you wake up every insecurity you have. Every doubt, fear, and past failure gets real mouthy when you gaze out over the horizon and attempt to better yourself. "Whoa, you think you can write a book? You think you can start a company? You think you can be a runner? At your age? With your background? No way."

The blank canvas you were planning to draw your potential on gets littered with obstacles, excuses, and challenges before you've even taken the first step.

Staring at that stubborn, stupid Vision Wall again, I decided to try something I'd never done before. Instead of looking forward, I looked back.

It wasn't a particularly strategic decision on my part; it was just the only option I had left. I wasn't living up to my potential in the present. The future wasn't providing any helpful answers. Guess what that left me? The past.

Looking back felt counterintuitive at first and flew in the face of every driftwood sign that told me, "Don't look back—you're not going that way." But the minute I did it, I knew I had stumbled onto a tool that would change my entire life. It turns out the path to full potential starts in the last place we all thought to look—the rearview mirror.

The Past Is the Future

Let's do a quick, one-question quiz.

Which activity would be easier for you?

1. Describe the best life you could achieve over the next twenty years.
2. Describe the best things that have happened to you over the last twenty years.

One is fantasy; the other is history.

One requires the courage to push through every fear, the vision-casting ability of Warren Buffett, the future-shaping creativity of Elon Musk, the unbridled positivity of Oprah, and the grit, persistence, and patience of a Navy SEAL.

The other requires a pen and a piece of paper.

I'd tried the first option for years and never had any success. I was zero for one million against the Vision Wall. Finally, sitting in the Augusta, Georgia, airport one afternoon, I decided to give the second option a spin.

I wrote "Best Moments" on a page in my notebook, and then I just started to write things down. I imagined that my past was a book and I had a bright yellow highlighter in my hand to easily identify what mattered the most.

I started my list in that small southern airport because I'd just experienced one of those moments and it was fresh in my mind. Speaking the night before to a sold-out crowd at the Augusta Metro Chamber of Commerce was the best. So I wrote that down in my notebook. I continued with some classic moments because that was the easiest way to get into the exercise. I scribbled:

- My wedding day.
- The birth of my two kids.
- Traveling to places like Santorini, Costa Rica, or New York at Christmastime.
- When I paid off my student loans.

Once the obvious ones were out of the way, some more unusual ones popped up:

- The time my friend and I ate a nine-pound lobster on Martha's Vineyard. It was the size of a carry-on suitcase and had to be opened with a circular saw.
- Petting my neighbor's dog Scout when I'm cooling down after a run.
- When one of my favorite authors, Steven Pressfield, sent me an encouraging note about a book I was writing.

Not all of the best moments I wrote down were singular events. Some were things that happen frequently.

- When a new month begins and I have a fresh thirty days at my disposal.
- Looking out the front door and seeing a package on our porch.
- Making my wife and kids laugh.

Some were just seemingly insignificant things that I personally like:

- Walking around Costco, especially at Christmastime.
- Sitting in a booth instead of a table at a restaurant.
- Seeing birds on our bird feeder.

I wrote down two dozen best moments in the airport that day and continued adding new ones as they came to mind over the next few days.

I didn't put any restrictions on what qualified as a best moment. I wanted it to feel like play, not a task. Whether I wanted to put down something major, such as "Getting the phone call that my book made the *New York Times* Bestseller list," or something minor, such as "The satisfaction of cleaning off the top of my desk at the end of the workweek," I could.

The list had only one rule: *It all counts.*

I fired that surly nightclub bouncer in my head who judges all my ideas harshly. There was no admission board reviewing applications. There was no HOA making sure the mailbox was the right color. Every moment of any size and any significance got in.

It was easy to create the list because you're guaranteed to win a game when you make the rules.

Your Past Is Full of Surprises

Even though I knew I'd learn at least a little from creating a Best Moments List, I didn't expect much from this exercise. I'm a goal nerd and have tried just about every technique of self-improvement, but for some reason this one was full of surprises.

The first surprise was that the list made me feel amazing. In hindsight, this revelation shouldn't have shocked me because it's impossible to make a list of your best moments and not feel better. I essentially told my head and my heart, "Please google up the best moments I've ever experienced in life. Find the friends, memories, and mementos I really care about the most."

I assume my head and my heart were both confused by this request because they tend to believe their job is to do just the opposite. They're undefeated at recalling mistakes I've made through the years and then replaying them at random times. It's like a constant series of surprise parties, except instead of "Happy Birthday!" the banner always says, "Remember that terrible thing you did?"

From wince-inducing things I shouldn't have said to mistakes I made at jobs I haven't worked at in years, my catalog of regrets is epic. Scientists call this *negativity bias*. It's just how our brains function. They overemphasize the negative and underemphasize the positive as a way to protect us against threats. "At the age of just eight months old, infants will turn

You're guaranteed to
win a game
when you
**MAKE THE
RULES.**

more quickly to look at an image of a snake rather than a frog, and a sad face rather than a happy face."[1]

But for the first time I was deliberately looking for moments that gave me joy. This made me feel like a bit of a rebel because for the last few decades modern psychology has been obsessed with sadness. In his book *Authentic Happiness*, Martin Seligman points out, "For every one hundred journal articles on sadness, there is just one on happiness."[2]

I experienced this in my own life in countless counseling and coaching sessions. In one group setting, I was instructed to draw a "trauma egg." On a big piece of paper, you draw an egg shape and then fill it in with doodles of everything horrible that's ever happened to you from birth to present day. In small groups with other married couples, when we "share our stories" at the beginning of a new group, it always ends up being a litany of the terrible things we've done or had done to us.

I'd never once been asked to create a list of my best moments in life, almost as if they didn't matter or have anything to teach me. The Best Moments List changed that. Instead of digging around in a coal mine for mistakes, it invited me to look inside a diamond mine for hope.

The second surprise I experienced through this exercise was that the list made me grateful. I won't bore you with the science on gratitude, but study after study has shown how good it is for you. I know that's true, and deep down that makes sense to me. But I've personally always had a hard time practicing gratitude without a plan. When someone says, "You should be grateful" or "You should have an abundance mindset," I always think, "Agreed, but how?"

I want practical, actionable steps. That's exactly what the Best Moments List gave me. The list became a shortcut to gratitude for me. Creating it made me grateful for so many things in life that I had either forgotten or taken for granted.

The third surprise was that the list taught me self-awareness, which is a superpower all its own. If you're not self-aware, you can't have real relationships, succeed at work, stay in shape, or accomplish any other goal that matters in life. How could you? Without self-awareness, you don't have an accurate picture of reality. The leader who thinks they're passionate is shocked to get fired one day for anger issues. The dad in his fifties is insulted when his doctor warns him he's dangerously overweight. The young woman in her late twenties is confused why she keeps attracting losers to date, never once wondering if she's the one who needs to change first.

Self-awareness is like when you hand a pair of full-spectrum glasses to someone who has been color-blind their entire life, or when you turn on cochlear implants and a toddler finally hears their mother's voice for the first time. Look at all the colors I can see! Listen to all the sounds I can hear! Check out the moments of life that make me come alive!

You can't tap into your potential if you don't know what you really care about. Guess what happens when you make a list of what you personally consider the best moments? You instantly figure out what you care about. The list is a fast pass to self-awareness.

The fourth surprise was that the list taught me mindfulness. That's a popular word right now, isn't it? We all want to be more present. We want to live in the moment, right? Do you know the easiest way to do that? Start paying attention to the things that are lighting you up. Being present is just learning to be nostalgic about the moment you're still in.

If you tell your head and your heart to look for awesome moments in your past, they naturally start looking for them in your present. As it's happening, you find yourself saying, "Oh, this moment is awesome, I should add that to my list!" You become present.

> **Being present is just learning to be nostalgic about the moment you're still in.**

Those four surprises alone were worth the price of admission—which, again, was a pen and a piece of paper—but the list wasn't done yet.

Back to the Future

As I read back through the list that had now grown to 170 items, I was struck by a profound thought that would change every day going forward: "I want more of that." I didn't want to stop at 170 items. I wanted the list to have a thousand items, ten thousand items, one million items!

That might feel far-fetched, but that's what happened when I reviewed the list. I couldn't help but think, "I want those moments to happen more often." Forget more often—can I make those moments happen all the time?

I'm a negative person by nature. I'm sarcastic. Despite believing in self-help, I'm highly skeptical of most of it. I was raised in New England with a wicked big chip on my shoulder about people who overpromise. But if I could pause that for a second—if I could suspend my disbelief for a minute—could I figure out a way to make my best moments the rule, not the exception?

Could I build a life where I leaped from one best moment to the next, deeply engaged in every part of my day, not just certain hours in certain weeks in certain months?

Could I do it on an ordinary Monday when there's not a trip to an exotic location or a big, obvious win on the calendar?

Could I live in my potential full-time instead of just visiting occasionally?

Could I ditch regret and make the rest of my life the best of my life?

If I could do that, could you do it too? And most importantly, could it really start with a list?

2

Build Your Best Moments List

I was trying to subtly woo you into making your own Best Moments List in that last chapter. I did a bit of a soft sell, didn't I? Want to be more self-aware? Want a quick way to learn gratitude and mindfulness? Hint, hint.

But if you've made it to chapter 2, you're no longer just a casual reader and are ready for a little bit of work, especially if the rewards are as good as I promised.

You've probably already thought of a few best moments in your life. I bet you've already taken your own highlighter to a few. Maybe you even wrote one down in the margin. It's an easy exercise once you get started. But to make it even easier, here are seven prompts that will spark your creativity as you search for your own best moments.

1. **Time speeds up or slows down when I _____.**
   When I write, sometimes I'll look up and be surprised at what time it is because it feels like the hours flew by. Sometimes it's just the opposite—I get up early and am surprised at how much I've accomplished when

35

I realize it's only 8 a.m. The time felt slow. Researchers at the Kavli Institute for Systems Neuroscience studied that exact phenomenon. They found that "by changing the activities you engage in, the content of your experience, you can actually change the course of the time-signal in LEC [the lateral entorhinal cortex portion of your brain] and thus the way you perceive time."[1] When you feel like time is speeding up or slowing down, it's not just a feeling, it's science.

Is there any activity you enjoy doing so much that it messes with your sense of time? The key word there is *enjoy*. Waiting in line at the DMV will slow down time, but you'd never add that to a Best Moments List. I've asked thousands of people this question over the years, and the answers come in every shape and size.[2] For Joe Wehmann, editing videos stops the clock. For Kathryn Marie, it's teaching. She says, "When I get in a groove lecturing about history for my students, I am sometimes shocked time has flown." For Jessica Benzing Smith, it's being in nature. She and her husband have walked outside 847 days in a row! For Michael Seewer it's cooking, and for Nikki Rimble it's playing the piano.

Editing videos is my nightmare. I can barely boil water. Piano lessons felt like something my parents made me do because they hated me. But this isn't my list. This is your list, so your answers will be different from mine and maybe from every example in this book.

To find a few of your own best moments, look to the clock. It will give you clues if you ask.

**2. The best job I ever had was _____,
and the reason I liked it so much was because**

_____**.**

Other than running my own company, the best job I
ever had was working for Dave Ramsey, a well-known
personal finance expert. The reason I liked it so much
was because we put on live events all over the country.
In the third month of my employment, he invited me
to speak to 8,000 people in an arena. That was 7,900
more people than I'd ever spoken to and was the BEST!

If you've never had a best job, make the prompt
even smaller. "My favorite part of my last job was
_____." At my last job when I lived in At-
lanta, we had a meeting every Wednesday where we
presented our current projects to the executives. I
liked the consistency of that deadline because it always helped shape my week. Live events and corporate
meetings are very different job experiences but would
both make my list.

3. Every time I see _____, I smile.
This one is fun to answer because it could be a person, place, or thing. Whenever I see my friend Rob
Sentell, I smile because he's hilarious and I know we'll
spend the entire time together laughing. Whenever
I see the rest stop on top of Monteagle, Tennessee, I
smile because it means I've left the traffic of Chattanooga and Atlanta behind me. The hill drops down,
the speed limit increases to 70, and now there's just a
straight, flat shot home to Nashville. Whenever I see

my Benchmade pocketknife, I smile because it makes me feel like a little boy again.

Kathryn Hanson said she always smiles when she watches her son navigate the world. One afternoon she saw him get off the bus and deliberately walk past the driveway so that he could step through a muddy ditch on his way to the house. It made her laugh that her rough-and-tumble little boy couldn't pass up a puddle. She added that moment to her list.

The next time you catch yourself smiling, look around and figure out why. There's a best moment there.

4. If I had a free hour today, I'd spend it _____.
I like watching videos on Instagram where influencers randomly give money to people in need. One guy starts his video by asking someone for a dollar, and if they give him one, he returns their kindness with $1,000. If that was me but I was able to give you a free hour instead, how would you spend it today? Don't look at your to-do list, the laundry that needs to be folded, or something you *should* do. What would you *want* to do with that hour? What's the first answer that really jumps out at you?

5. If I won $163 million in the lottery, I'd turn _____ into a millionaire too.
That's a very specific amount of money, but only because it really happened. In October 2011, Dave Dawes and his girlfriend Angela won £101 million, roughly $163 million. In addition to donating to charities,

they decided to make a few friends and family members millionaires too. "We've drawn up a list of 15 to 20 people . . . anyone who has helped us through our lives," Dave said.[3] Instead of just trying to think which relationships you'd add to your Best Moments List, think about who you'd give a million dollars to.

6. **This might sound like I'm bragging, but three of my greatest accomplishments are: 1.**_____ **2.**_____ **3.**_____.

We don't have time to waste on shyness or the fear of being labeled a show-off when we're building a Best Moments List. If you accomplished something you're proud of, if you did a little private fist pump in the car when you drove home from a successful meeting, or if you keep thinking about the day when all the pieces came together on a project, write that down. We have so few avenues for celebrating our wins in life that this one can be hard at first. Leslie McQuiston, a pediatric urologist, wrote down, "I'm a mom and a surgeon—there, I'm owning it. I'm not embarrassed by it." Can you imagine a world where a mom has been told she should be embarrassed by owning those two accomplishments? I can. It's called "our world." Don't hold back on this one. Own it.

7. **When I scroll through my camera roll on my phone, I always get inspired when I see**

_____.

Don't just try to imagine what encourages you; go back through your photos and see what moments you cared about enough to take a picture. I guarantee there are some you've forgotten. Erin Clark, an analyst, found that Facebook Memories made it easy for her to put together a Best Moments List. Don't be afraid to turn to technology for a little bit of help.

Those prompts will be enough to get you up and running, but if you really want to geek out on your list, you can grab twenty more prompts and thirty examples of what I put on my list at JonAcuff.com/list.

You can also create your own prompts.

Tahis Blue, one of the research participants, liked my list of questions but told me, "In the long season of parenting toddlers, it can be really challenging to remember awesome moments and look forward to new ones." So she wrote two of her own questions to build her list: "(1) When do you feel or have you felt the most joy with your kids? (2) When have you felt or what makes you feel connected to your husband?"

Another way to expand your list is to ask friends if there's anything they would add. Remember, I didn't have a eureka moment and magically discover that I liked Volkswagen GTIs. I asked my wife Jenny what she thought, and she helped me. All you need to do is text one friend and say something like this:

> I'm working on an exercise with an author named Jon Acuff called a Best Moments List, where I create a massive list of the things that light me up. They can be memories from my past, hobbies I love, skills that come naturally to me, or anything at all that gives me joy. He says sometimes they're hard for us to notice because it's like we're standing so close to the painting of our

> lives that we can't really see the entire canvas. As a friend who has a wider perspective of my life, is there anything you'd add to my list?

If you're an introvert and that last suggestion made your skin crawl, no problem. Build your list in the way that works for you. I first wrote down my best moments in a notebook before typing them all into a Word document because I tend to be a kinesthetic learner and appreciate a tactile experience. If you'd prefer to draw them out, talk them into an audio file you get transcribed, or collage them with art supplies, go for it. The method you use doesn't really matter as long as you end up with a collection of moments that gives you a sneak peek into you. Bryan Robinson wrote his best moments on Post-it notes that he kept by his computer keyboard. Why? "So I can easily add to it, see it, and continue to be encouraged by it!" he said.

I wasn't the only one benefiting from this simple tool. When I launched a six-week study of the Best Moments List with more than 250 people, I was encouraged that even though they all used different collection methods, the results were the same. When I challenged the participants to come up with thirty items, Eric Recker, a dentist in Pella, Iowa, blew past that number. "My list keeps growing," he told me. "It's well over 150 items. I am having a huge realization. This life that I have put so much pressure on myself and have struggled to just let myself enjoy, I have made so many amazing memories and moments along the way. It really is a great life. And I am already finding ways to have more of these moments. The list is already life-changing, and I believe the best is yet to come!"

Eric turned potential into a goal, used his Best Moments List as a helpful tool, and was surprised by the results.

That wasn't everyone's immediate response, of course.

Veronica said, "This list has been challenging for me because I get so stuck in my head all the time that I often don't realize the 'amazing' moments."

Rita said, "I know that I have several best moments, but my tendency is to devalue things that relate to me."

Carol said, "It wasn't easy at first; I am pessimistic by nature."

Those are all perfectly fine responses because the Best Moments List is the opposite of everything you were taught to do:

Don't boast.

Focus on your trauma.

Look forward to figure out your future.

Thinking about yourself is selfish.

For many people, this exercise will feel very foreign, but it was fun to watch everyone who struggled with it make progress. The last time I checked in with Carol, she was killing her list: "Once I got going, it got easier. I keep adding to the list. Yesterday it was lunch with a friend whom I haven't seen in a few months. Today I picked up my grandson from school and we played farming with the toy tractors I saved from when my son was little. This very moment is best because I'm sitting with my husband listening to the birds and the waterfall." She added three things to her list without batting an eye.

The key with an exercise like this is to remember what I told you in chapter 1: fire the bouncer. Everyone gets in this nightclub. There's no velvet rope, no guest list, and no dress code. You get to put anything on your Best Moments List.

How many moments will be on your list? I don't know. There's not a perfect number you should be shooting for. It's also not the type of exercise you finish. I added more than 170 the first few weeks I tried it, and now I add a new moment every other day or so.

The Best Moments List is the opposite of everything you were taught to do.

If the only thing the Best Moments List accomplished was teaching gratitude, self-awareness, mindfulness, and happiness, it would be the greatest piece of paper since the US Constitution. But when I spent a little more time looking at it, I realized I hadn't even scratched the surface of what it was capable of.

Do you remember those cheesy 3D posters from the 1990s? The ones that if you stared at them long enough, a unicorn on a sailboat would suddenly appear? That's what happened when I really looked at the list—only the four things I saw were way better than a unicorn.

3

Conquer the Future
by Categorizing the Past

I've never filled out a personality assessment honestly.

I've taken many of them. Throw any acronym at me—DISC, MBTI, FFM—I've probably knocked it out at an offsite for one of my jobs, but I've never filled one out honestly.

That's OK, because neither have you. No one has. Despite my best attempts, some degree of "should" always slips in.

I should answer this question a different way.

I should check this box if I want to be seen as a leader.

I should pick this option if I want to get promoted.

I should care more about listening skills, so I should choose this response.

It's impossible to not fudge at least a few of your answers as you decide who you would like to be but actually aren't yet.

I took one personality test that asked, "Have you ever felt like you could be a stand-up comedian?" It was clear that I was supposed to answer "No." I'm not sure why they picked on that profession specifically, but there was no way I was going to have some manager reviewing the answer to that question in a salary discussion with other leaders at the company. "By his own admittance, Jon said he could be a stand-up comedian. I think we should demote him, or at the very least give him a smaller cubicle by the bathroom."

Even if you don't think you're funny, so many of the questions about who you are can go so many different ways that it's hard to get an accurate picture of yourself. That's why the Best Moments List is so powerful.

It's not a fictional list of what you might care about. It's not a fantasy about what you could enjoy someday. It's not a portrait built from the hopes you've been carrying for years but haven't acted on. It's a snapshot of who you really are. And whether you've got thirty moments on it or three thousand, four patterns will emerge that will show you the future if you look hard enough.

I don't know what's on your list, but I know every single moment will fit into one of four categories:

1. Experience
2. Accomplishment
3. Relationship
4. Object

Those four categories have been driving the best parts of your life for years. They've just been waiting for you to notice.

What do they mean?

Every single moment will fit into one of <mark>four categories:</mark>

1. Experience
2. Accomplishment
3. Relationship
4. Object

Experience = A best moment you took part in

It could be an experience that only happened once, like a trip to Hawaii. It could be an experience that happens often, like walking into your favorite local coffee shop. You light up the second you go through those doors. It could be a significant experience, like getting asked to the prom in high school, or something as small as how a new book smells when you get it. You guys don't smell new books? You're missing out. That's an experience.

Accomplishment = A best moment achieved through your effort

This is a goal or task you succeeded at. Signing a book deal is an accomplishment. Getting up early and beating all the traffic on your drive to work in Atlanta is an accomplishment. Getting a raise is an accomplishment. Cleaning your office on a Friday afternoon so that it's ready for you on Monday morning is an accomplishment. Going to the gym is an accomplishment. There's a win involved no matter how small or big.

Seeing a bald eagle near my house was an experience because those aren't common in Nashville, but there wasn't any effort on my part to make that happen. If, however, I joined a bird-watching club, read books about whooping cranes, and traveled to another state to experience their migratory patterns, that would be an accomplishment.

Relationship = A moment another person made best

This is a moment that was made best by your interaction with someone else. If you removed that person, the moment wouldn't make the list. For example, going out to dinner with friends every Wednesday night is a relationship moment. If I went out to dinner by myself, even at the same restaurant we usually all go to, I wouldn't list it as a best moment, so therefore the people are what matters most. If someone else is involved in the moment, it's a relationship moment.

Object = A physical item you think is the best
This fourth category is slightly different from the first three. Simply put, this is a physical thing that brings a smile to your face. A new pair of running sneakers is an object. A favorite pair of noise-canceling headphones that make travel so much better is an object. A car that you're excited to walk back to in the parking lot after running an errand is an object. A visual timer you use to focus during the day is an object.

Take a quick look at your list. Every single item will fit in one of those categories. I've done this with hundreds of people and thousands of best moments, and it always works. The four categories are undefeated.

Why does understanding the categories matter? Because when you understand them, your list transforms from a task about the past into a tool for the future. It's like finally seeing the individual ingredients for your favorite meal and realizing you can cook it again and again.

Armed with that realization, I started to label my list.

The day I skied alone in Utah = Experience
I skied alone, so it's not a relationship moment. I didn't

succeed at anything, so it's not an accomplishment. If I loved that moment because I had tracked my total vertical feet with an app, it would have been an accomplishment, but that's not what I wrote down. I don't own that ski resort, so it's not an object. Skiing was an experience.

Seeing the headlights in our driveway when our kids come home = Relationship

Have you ever taught a kid how to drive? Terrifying. It's shocking how little they know about this 3,000-pound weapon you're about to send them down the highway in at 70 miles per hour. Seeing my kids come home from a friend's house means they've made it back safely. That's definitely a best moment for me.

Finishing a whole notebook of ideas = Accomplishment

If you're a paper person, have you ever made it to the very last page of a notebook? So satisfying. Unlike all the previous times when I wrote twenty pages deep, got distracted by a new one, and abandoned the notebook, this time I completed it. That's a real accomplishment for someone who had to write a whole book called *Finish* just to teach himself how to transform from a chronic starter into a consistent finisher.

Doing the donut run with my youngest daughter = Relationship

Have you ever eaten four donuts while also running a mile as fast as you can? I'm talking cheap, thick, grocery-store glazed donuts, the kind that make your mouth feel greasy just reading this sentence. I have. It was horrible. It made me hate donuts for a month. Why is it on my Best Moments List? Because I ran it with my daughter McRae.

Showing up to meetings prepared = Accomplishment

Meetings made a few cameos on my Best Moments List. For example, item number 132: "When a meeting ends early or, better yet, gets canceled." When I get fifteen or thirty minutes back in my day, I feel so relieved. While I'm not a huge fan of meetings, I do love showing up to them prepared. I particularly enjoy having answers to the questions I know people are going to ask. That's an accomplishment.

If it sounds like it was easy for me to label my list, that's only because it was. It's the clearest tool you'll ever use to understand what you care about. Objects are easy to find. You won't confuse a favorite pair of Jordans with an accomplishment. Relationships are simple to identify too. If there's even one other person in the moment, it's a relationship moment. Accomplishments and experiences can get a little foggy, but was your effort the star of the moment or just something that made a cameo? Hiking a trail is an experience. Hiking a trail faster than you ever have is an accomplishment. Hiking it with a friend is a relationship. A pine cone you picked up on the trail and keep on your desk is an object.

You don't even have to write out the whole word. Just go through your list and put E, A, R, or O beside each item, then add them up. When I did that, my list broke down like this:

61 accomplishments

59 experiences

35 relationships

15 objects

A few things stood out to me about those results.

1. I love accomplishments far more than I knew.

I grew up with a church experience where success was often viewed as a bad thing, and therefore accomplishments were something to either downplay or be outright ashamed of. Even if that's not your exact situation, our culture doesn't encourage being proud of what you've done. Post something good that you achieved online and someone will inevitably comment with #HumbleBrag. Misery loves company and encourages the sharing of that in social media, but we have a much harder time celebrating when people are winning.

When I studied my Best Moments List, it was hard to deny an honest truth: I find accomplishments very motivational. Even in personality tests like the popular Enneagram, I used to test as the fun-loving, extroverted Seven, the Enthusiast. But as I've dug deeper into who I really am and have learned from exercises like this, it seems like I'm more of a Three, the Achiever. I'm driven and ambitious. This wasn't a surprise to friends, who often tease me about my obsession with goals, but seeing how much I loved accomplishments initially caught me off guard.

2. **Relationships are important but not motivational.**
Only 20 percent of my best moments involved other people. I'm not a loner by any stretch of the imagination, and I love people, but I'm far more introverted than I originally knew. What confused me was that my job, public speaking, appears like an extroverted activity, but on closer inspection, it's not. Everyone might be looking at me during a speech, but I'm the only one with a microphone. I'm alone on that stage, in complete control of the moment. I'm not in a band, creating something new with other people onstage at the same time. I have a much harder time being on a twenty-minute panel with five other presenters than doing a ninety-minute keynote by myself because a panel requires interacting with other people, which is true extroversion. The list reminded me I'm an introvert.

3. **Objects do next to nothing for me.**
Maybe that's why every time I try to use an object as a reward for finishing a goal, I lose motivation midway. For example, I purchased an expensive print of a fancy car a few years ago. My plan was to tie it to some business goal and then cut up the picture into dozens of pieces. Every time I hit a financial number, I'd paste

another piece up on a piece of whiteboard and rebuild the vehicle. When I finished the last portion of the goal, I'd buy the car. Do you know where that poster is right now? In the tube it came in. I haven't done anything with it because the truth is, I don't really care about objects. That's why they represented less than 10 percent of my favorite moments.

4. Social media didn't make the list once.
One of the fun parts of the Best Moments List is that you'll be surprised at what's missing. I wrote down more than 170 of my best moments, and not one of them involved social media. So then why am I spending seven hours a week on Instagram? Isn't it strange to give almost a full workday of time to something I don't even consider best?

As you review your list, what relationships didn't you mention? What experiences aren't important to you? What objects do you think you're supposed to have but don't really enjoy? If they didn't make your list, why are they still in your life?

A large percent of readers won't end up tallying their list, and I get it. I don't like when books give me dozens of tasks to complete, as if I've signed up for a class and not just picked up a book to scratch a curiosity. I don't like workbooks that pretend to be books, either, but this isn't one. If you create and categorize a Best Moments List, you'll have more than just a piece of paper full of memories. You'll have a foundation that will help you build on your potential for years to come.

A Warning and a Promise

When I shared the Best Moments List activity with research participants, live audiences, and anyone who would even remotely make eye contact with me during the writing of this book, something unexpected would happen: people understood the concept but often didn't think they had permission to try it. We've all been so trained to focus on weaknesses to fix at work, problems to address at home, and shortcomings to deal with in school that searching for the best moments in life, the little personal wins, felt foreign to them at first.

So I warn you—that might happen to you initially as well. If there's a dragon on the doorstep that would prevent you from ever taking the first step of this journey, we might as well address it. I assure you that you do indeed have permission to build your own Best Moments List. And when you do, I promise I know exactly what will happen for you next: the best moments from your past will help you improve your present and plan your future.

A best moment is when your vision and your reality overlap. It's when how you hoped life could be actually matches how life is. It's when who you want to be lines up with who you are. Simply put, your dream matches your day. That's what every best moment has in common—your vision and your reality coming together.

Sometimes reality even exceeds your vision of what was possible. I could imagine what the sweeping view overlooking the Pacific Ocean at an open-air restaurant in Costa Rica would look like, but my vision couldn't do it justice. The photos online didn't do it justice. My description right now—even if

I told you what the island in the harbor looked like and how surprising it was to see a family of squirrel monkeys commuting across the tops of the jungle canopy—doesn't do it justice. Reality was the only thing that could capture that moment. It's why we invented the saying "You had to be there."

And you were there. For dozens, maybe hundreds of moments, you experienced something that made time slow down. A situation where you wanted to plant your feet, root yourself right into the ground, and never leave.

We've all been there. We've all tasted a bit of the best.

But we've also experienced the *itch* of potential. Why is it an itch?

Because potential is the gap between your vision and your reality—when how you thought life would be doesn't match how life is yet.

The best news is that potential cannot be wasted. It can't be lost. It can't be canceled.

Why?

Because you are not an acorn.

> **Potential is the gap between your vision and your reality.**

Picking up acorns when I see them is perhaps the most old-man thing I do, along with saying things like "We really needed this rain," and "It's not heavy, it's just awkward" whenever I lift something, and "We got here in the nick of time" whenever a line forms behind me.

I can't help picking up an acorn, though, because it's the perfect picture of potential. Inside that half-ounce acorn is an eighty-foot oak tree. Inside that one-inch kingdom is ten thousand pounds of timber. Inside that tiny seed is a log cabin. Inside a handful of acorns is an entire forest. Scoop up a few hundred and you're holding a mile of the Appalachian Trail.

The potential of an acorn is phenomenal, but it is temporary. Acorns last a few months, sometimes even a few years, but eventually their moment passes. Their potential is gone. There's not a thing you can do to reanimate that acorn. There's not a step, a technique, a goal, a resolution that will awaken what was once hidden inside it. The acorn is over.

But you are not an acorn.

Your potential cannot be ruined. It cannot be ended. It cannot be damaged beyond repair. Your potential can, however, be ignored. For a month, for a year, for a lifetime if you're not careful. But it's always available if you choose to work at it.

You're always one day away from starting a new forest.

You're always one day away from starting a new forest. You're always one moment away from unlocking the treasure chest that is your potential. You're always one decision away from tapping into the person you secretly always knew you could be.

The Best Moments List is the first tool we'll use to do that, but it's time to move beyond our past. It's time to live in the present and win the future. To do that, you'll have to deal with the most difficult person you've ever met.

4

Trick the Hardest Person to Change

The hardest person I deal with every day is me.

If I invest a few hundred dollars and a few hours a week in the gym, I get to live longer. That's an amazing return on investment. But most days I don't want to go to the gym.

If I write every day, I get to publish books, which means my kids can go to college without debt. But most days I don't feel like writing.

If I reach out to friends, lifting them up when they're discouraged and asking for encouragement when I am, I get to have deep, long-term relationships. Researchers at Harvard have studied social isolation for nearly eighty years and found that it is "associated with a 50 to 90 percent higher risk of early death."[1] Even knowing that, on most days I isolate myself and am frustrated when someone calls me instead of just texting.

If I brush and floss my teeth faithfully, I won't need to have root canals. But most days I act like it's the greatest hardship in the world.

I know the massive rewards a little bit of work will generate—long life, money for college and retirement, strong friendships, root-canal-free years—but none of it moves the needle. Putting together my Best Moments List reminded me of my potential, but I'm a hard person to keep in motion. My Instagram bio lists my official title as "Motivational Speaker," but most days I find it challenging to motivate me, never mind you.

The reason is obvious: I don't like doing difficult things because they're difficult.

It's far easier to not go to the gym, not write a book, not engage with friends, and not floss. Sheer willpower, grit, and discipline might sustain me for a week or two, but eventually I'm able to talk myself out of it.

I'm the most persuasive person I've ever met. When people say, "The only one standing in your way is you," I think, "I know. That guy is impossible!"

If you had a friend who swore they wanted to live up to their full potential but then ignored all your advice, you'd be frustrated at that friend. If for months, maybe years, they told you today was the day and then they promptly did the opposite of what you suggested, you'd be angry at that friend.

If I were my client, I would've fired me a long time ago. If this were a dating relationship, I would've faked an emergency phone call and bolted in the middle of the first date. If I were anyone else, dealing with me wouldn't be worth the hassle, but there's no getting rid of me. This is the only me I've got. You've got one you. I've got one me.

You're the most

PERSUASIVE
PERSON

you've ever met.

I wouldn't mind my aggressive resistance to change if creating new best moments weren't so painfully simple. It would be one thing if tapping into my full potential was some terribly complicated task, but it's not.

If you want to hold your published book in your hands, which is certainly a best moment, there are some very obvious steps. If you want to enjoy the delightful endorphins of exercise, a best moment you can have daily, there are a million resources at your fingertips. If you want to have friends who are invested in your life, a best moment that makes you feel connected to a community, there are easy actions. Most of the things we want to accomplish in life aren't mysterious or complex.

For almost every goal, I can see what I need to do to accomplish it, but I have a second obstacle that's even worse than the Vision Wall. My "stuck self," that portion of me that makes change a chore, is incredibly strong. Despite my best attempts to inspire myself, the results were always the same: short-term success followed by long bouts of inaction.

I tried that approach to life for four decades. What can I say? I like to be thorough in making sure something isn't working. As I mentioned, I'm a late bloomer. It took me until my midthirties to even know I had potential, and until my midforties in the Augusta airport to start doing something about it.

I'm always slow to the party, but once I get there, my favorite thing is to tell everyone else where it is. I point out the fastest paths, share every obstacle to avoid, and reveal the hard-fought lessons so you don't have to fight for them too. Then I put it all in the smallest, simplest invitation I can create, which is usually in the form of a book just like this to make sure you also get to the party.

When I reviewed my Best Moments List for anything I might have missed, an experience I hadn't thought about for fifteen years jumped out at me, and suddenly the game was on.

The Revolution Will Be Blogged

In 2008, I started my third blog. There was no real calculation involved in this decision, no strategy or plan. I came up with a silly joke I wanted to write about that wasn't even an original concept. I figured I would explore it on a blog for a few weeks before getting bored and giving up. I wrote twenty posts, emailed the URL to a hundred friends, and didn't expect anything to happen.

Eight days later, four thousand people showed up.

I wish I could tell you exactly how it happened, but the only people who say they have a formula for making something go viral are trying to sell you that formula. Despite my complete lack of technical skills, a URL with a typo in it, and no clear direction, the blog gained momentum. A few weeks in, I decided to put my foot on the gas pedal as hard as I could because for the very first time in my life, I peeked behind the curtain and discovered a powerful truth: *this is just a game.*

I could see the pieces and the other players and understood what it would take to win the blogging game. More than that, the scorecard was obvious and I loved watching it. I liked how it felt to see my blog traffic go up on Google Analytics. I liked watching the list of countries where the site was being read climb. I enjoyed the dozens and then hundreds of comments from readers. I liked all the tiny little daily wins this blog added to my life. It was a best moment that I actually recognized in real time, not just in hindsight, and I wanted more of that.

It's fun to win games. If I wanted to win this one, all I had to do was turn it into a goal and lean into the rules. They were really easy. The more I wrote, the more I could post. The more I posted, the more people would read. The more I shared links to posts, the more people would visit the blog. The more people who visited the blog, the more comments I would get. The more I commented back, the more interaction I would get with readers.

It all felt so obvious to me. I had figured out the Matrix, and the bullets weren't bullets—they were just lines of code.

If I'd told my stuck self, "I need you to write two million words, start getting up at 5 a.m., stop watching TV so you can focus on new posts, and create Excel spreadsheets of other bloggers you should connect with," the immediate answer would have been, "Nope."

If I'd told my stuck self, "If you'll stay faithful to this and approach it with consistency, you'll end up moving to Nashville, writing nine books, speaking at a Range Rover event with Wyclef Jean, and putting your kids through college with your ideas," the immediate answer would have been a panic attack. There's no way I could have handled that much pressure or expectation on each ridiculous blog post I was writing at the beginning.

But I didn't do that to myself. All I did was play a game, and games are easy.

You've got at least eighteen years of experience under your belt with games. You learned how to play games before you could even walk: peekaboo, hide-and-seek, tag. Teachers used games to teach us how to read in elementary school. Coaches used them to inspire us in middle school. And in high school, games kept us alive.

I recently hosted a speaking engagement at 3:30 a.m. That's not the usual time I like to speak, but this wasn't a usual event. It was a game.

A few years ago, parents and teachers realized that graduation night was a dangerous moment for teenagers. Teen traffic accidents tend to increase from April to July, or prom to Fourth of July. Right in the middle of that season was graduation. They couldn't make every night safer, but they could focus on one particular hot spot.

Instead of increasing "Don't drink and drive" messaging or hosting additional school assemblies that preached against distracted driving, the administration came up with a game. Project Graduation is an all-nighter held at the school right after the graduation ceremony. From 10 p.m. to 5 a.m. the kids are entertained and rewarded with prizes. Rather than slingshot hundreds of graduates into the night after a moment they've been building toward for eighteen years, the school made the craziest game they could think of and then invited them to play. My job was to help give out the prizes. Super easy crowd, by the way, teenagers at 3:30 a.m.

It works because games work.

Playing a game is a lot easier than "living up to your full potential." Just that phrase invokes an angry high school principal who has called you down to the office to tell you, "You're wasting your life, Johnson!" With certain dreams it's easy to get your identity all wrapped up into your accomplishments.

Writing a book, launching a business, getting in shape—goals like that often carry baggage and emotions. But a game is just a game. It's something I play. I expect it to have ups and downs. Every game does.

Games also make discipline a lot easier. Consistency is hard. Willpower is hard. Self-control is hard. You know what's not? Playing a game. When I have a game, with a clear win that I'm genuinely excited about and the promise of a new best moment, it becomes a lot easier to focus. I don't have to white-knuckle my week trying to avoid wasting time on Instagram. I just have to find a game that I love so much that the joy of playing it makes me want to steal time away from other areas of my life so that I can play more. Distractions lose their allure in the light of a good game.

I didn't start getting up at 5 a.m. to write my blog because I'd unlocked some Mark Wahlberg work ethic. I just had something I loved so much that even sleep took a back seat. You don't have to force yourself to play a game you enjoy; it becomes a magnet that pulls you toward it with its own momentum.

In a 70,000-page study dating back to the 1970s, professor Mihaly Csikszentmihalyi (Me-high Cheek-sent-me-high) found that "feelings of concentration, creativity and satisfaction were reported more often at work than at home."[2] How can this be true in a culture that all too often demonizes the office and serves "Sunday scaries" drink specials in bars because people don't want to return to work on Monday morning?

Csikszentmihalyi says, "What often passes unnoticed is that work is much more like a game than most other things we do during the day."[3] At work, there are clear goals, agreed-upon rules, feedback, and an environment that encourages you to use your skills to overcome challenges. In other words, "work tends to have the structure of other intrinsically rewarding activities that provide flow, such as games."[4] Whether you use Csikszentmihalyi's concept of flow or use the word *potential*, the result is the same: games make the best moments easier to achieve.

Games make the best moments easier to achieve.

I experienced fleeting bursts of potential at work because someone else built a game I could play. When I went in the building each day, I was playing Home Depot's game or Staples' game or AutoTrader.com's game. The jobs weren't always amazing— they were still jobs, after all. But there were best moments for me at those companies because there were games at those companies.

The reason I was living out of my potential with my blog was that it was the first game I built on my own. That's what I discovered when I asked the question, "Why did I work so hard at that goal?"

Up until that moment in life, I had coasted. I was the picture of unused potential. I had eight full-time jobs in the first twelve years of adulthood. I was charismatic enough to get hired, but the minute I'd get bored, I'd quit and find a different job. My career didn't have any momentum because before the ink on the business card had even dried I'd be leaving again.

My relationships weren't going any better. When I asked my future father-in-law for his daughter's hand in marriage, he said, "No." Worst moment in a Waffle House ever. He remembers that the Eagles' "Desperado" was playing on the jukebox, which is an oddly appropriate soundtrack for that conversation. Twenty-two years of marriage later, we're great friends, and now that I have two teenage daughters of my own, I completely agree with his initial response. Saying no to me was 100 percent the right decision because I was headed nowhere.

That's the backdrop to me starting my blog. That's the setup I'm walking into that experience with. So then why did it work? Fifteen years after I started it, asking that question really challenged me. That foray into my potential changed the arc of my entire life. If I could trick my stuck self into massive amounts of action by turning blogging into a game, were there other areas where I could do the same thing?

Were other people already doing this too?

Turns out the answer is "yes" and "yes."

The Most Productive Trick of All

Dara Schuler's kids don't want to do chores and schoolwork.

Is that the least surprising sentence you've ever read in a book? What kid does? I often worry about my kids' eyesight because they apparently can't see the dishwasher. Even though it's located seventeen inches from the sink, they keep refusing to load their dirty dishes in it. I know they can see the sink because that's where they pile the remains of the day, but that last seventeen inches to the dishwasher is impossible for them. Maybe they need Lasik.

Dara could lean into discipline with her kids: "You have to clean up your room as a member of this family." Dara could appeal to their sense of duty: "School is your job, and homework is part of doing that job well." Dara could even use a little bit of guilt to see if that helped: "I work all day and make dinner every night—all I'm asking is that you tidy up the bathroom a little bit." She could try all of those approaches, but none of them will work long-term.

So instead, she tricks her kids with the greatest, most effective trick for improvement that's ever been invented: a game.

How does she do it? I'll let Dara tell you in her own words.

"On a giant flip chart piece of paper, I write various chores, schoolwork, and fun activities. Then I cover each one with a Post-it. The kids then uncover one and go do the item, not knowing which category it will be. Sometimes it's two chores in a row, sometimes it's two fun things." The items on the sheet are random. "I would even throw in 'give mom a high five' and 'do twenty jumping jacks.' They loved it AND it kept me from being the bad guy because I wasn't giving directions, rather the paper told them what to do next."

Dara might describe her chart as a craft project, but it's actually a brilliant game. It's visual, simple, and surprising. There's an element of chance to it that the brain loves. Dopamine is often misidentified as the "happiness hormone," as if you get more of it when something good happens to you. But that's not how it really works. "Dopamine activity is not a marker of pleasure. It is a reaction to the unexpected—to possibility and anticipation."[5]

Dopamine is driven by what scientists call "reward prediction errors." If you thought a meeting was going to last ninety minutes and it ends thirty minutes early, your prediction was wrong and you get a burst of dopamine. When your sales commission this month is higher than you expected, you get a hit of dopamine. When you pull off a Post-it on a chore chart and instead of a chore it says, "Play your favorite video game for fifteen minutes," you get a hit of dopamine.

This always happens when you tap into more of your potential. Why? Because the outcome is never exactly what you expected it would be. When I wrote my first book, I couldn't have predicted that receiving a foreign edition in the mail would become one of the biggest best moments. No author is cocky or creative enough to think, "I bet someday I'll have a Russian edition of my book that has a singing lobster climbing a mountain on the cover." But that's exactly what happened. (A mountain-climbing, singing lobster is a Russian idiom to describe things that are impossible, similar to the American English phrase "When pigs fly.")

Dopamine is driven by what scientists call "reward prediction errors."

When you work at your potential, there are always surprises. "That happy error is what launches dopamine into action. It's not the extra time or the extra money themselves. It's the thrill of the unexpected good news."[6] It's the joy of playing a game instead of doing a chore, and it works for kids and adults.

This Shouldn't Have Worked, but It Did

April Bacon—real name, and yes, I'm really happy about that—had a challenge much harder than just chores. When she was twenty-three years old, she was put in charge of fourteen employees who were all age fifty or older. "They resented my presence," April says bluntly.

It wasn't just April's age that bothered coworkers—it was her mission. She had been hired to automate all the projects, change what the employees were doing, and eliminate them if possible. In order to do that, she was assigned a weekly scorecard that she was measured against. The measurements included data points like how long the employees were on the phone and how fast they produced documents. This was an impossible task for April.

Just imagine, you're not even old enough to rent a car yet, you're managing people your parents' age, and the goal is motivating them to move faster so that you can prove you don't need so many of them in the department. I got a little sweaty just writing that sentence.

The employees had every incentive not to help April, and she knew it. "They had no desire to help me succeed but all the desire to see me fail. They were intentionally slowing down." When she shared this story with me, there was one word she capitalized in her explanation: UNTIL. Everyone was working against her, she said, "UNTIL I made it a game."

Everything shifted at that moment. "I made fourteen scorecards, one for each of them, that directly mirrored mine. On Fridays, if they showed improvement in any metric of seven total, they got a raffle ticket for each metric. The raffle tickets were then drawn at the end of the month for two $100 gift cards."

Did the employees take to the game right away? Of course not. Remember, if they played the game well, they might lose their jobs. "They squawked when I announced the program and asked if I thought they were elementary kids," April said. "But guess who knocked on my door for their tickets every Friday and were coming asking me to help them be faster? They were."

By the end of the eight months, the team had automated half of their work, the staff had been reduced, and April was promoted with a 26 percent pay raise, the biggest raise her director had handed out in forty years. "We doubled the efficiency for $200 a month," April said. "I even persuaded my boss to foot the bill. She said it was the easiest $1,600 she'd ever authorized!"

If you're a fan of bureaucracy and inefficiency, you probably rooted against April in that story, but the power of the principle remains.

Games make it easier to do things you don't naturally want to do.

I don't naturally want to go to the gym.

I don't naturally want to write books.

I don't naturally want to floss.

But if I want to live up to my full potential and enjoy all the best moments that come when I do, I need to do a whole lot of things I might not want to do at first.

So do you.

If you've read one hundred books like this and one hundred didn't work, it's not because you're lazy. You just have the same phenomenal obstacle I have. It's called your stuck self. You've got an opponent who is able to marshal every memory, every emotion, every failed previous attempt, every custom-tailored temptation each time you try to visit the Potential Zone.

You think Instagram is good at personalizing the ads it sends you? It only listens to a *few* of your conversations. You, on the other hand, have heard every conversation you've ever had. In war, the side with the best intel usually wins. Imagine if one side spent every single day with the other, for twenty, thirty, even fifty years. Could they correctly anticipate and counteract every move?

Of course.

That's what we're up against.

We beat the Vision Wall with the Best Moments List by looking to our past, not our future. But our stuck selves won't give up that easy. If we're going to really enjoy our full potential, we're going to need a whole lot of new tricks.

THE ZONES

5

Navigate the Three Performance Zones

I am a goal nerd. I love goals like some people love wine, bird-watching, gardening, or video games.

One year I read a hundred books. One year I ran a thousand miles. One year I hired a table tennis coach because I wanted to see how good I could get at Ping-Pong. Raise your hand if you've ever hired a Team USA–sanctioned elderly man to throw hundreds of Ping-Pong balls at you in a rental property while yelling, "Kill! Kill! Kill!" Any hands raise? Probably not.

I'm a goal nerd. You might not be, but you are a high performer. How do I know? Because lazy people don't read books like this. They don't even know this section of the bookstore exists. Low performers don't voluntarily read books about tapping into their full potential. Only high performers do that, so allow me to congratulate you for being a high performer.

Before we celebrate too loudly, though, I must share one warning. Being a high performer doesn't automatically make you a high achiever. We all know plenty of people who are capable of sporadic bursts of high performance but never figure out how to turn all that motion into high achievement. I discovered the reason this happens after twelve years of helping thousands of people with their goals. High performers bounce between three different zones:

1. The Comfort Zone
2. The Potential Zone
3. The Chaos Zone

In the Comfort Zone, we've disconnected from our vision for our lives. We've settled for the familiar, bought the lie that dreaming is for other people, and decided that the safe repetitiveness of being stuck is better than the risk of stretching for more. There are no actions, no goals, and no progress, but we rarely notice the inertia because it's so comfortable. It's an amazing place to visit but ultimately a terrible place to live.

Though the Comfort Zone gets a lot more press, the Chaos Zone is the one that traps more high performers. Have you ever tried too many goals at once? Have you ever listened to a podcast that got you fired up and made you want to change every part of your life all at once? Do you have a habit of overscheduling your day, overpromising what you can deliver, and overestimating how fast you can get something done? Have you ever tried to start a side hustle, lose ten pounds, be a better spouse, earn a raise at your day job, figure out crypto, and meditate more—all in the same weekend? That's the Chaos Zone.

High performers bounce between three zones:

1. The Comfort Zone
2. The Potential Zone
3. The Chaos Zone

The Potential Zone is in the middle of those two extremes. It's the Goldilocks Zone—not too hot, not too cold, just right. You don't yo-yo between never dieting and weighing the ounces of green matcha protein powder on a scale designed for Tour de France cyclists. You make steady, joyful progress on a handful of goals you care about. Each day, as you intentionally invest in best moments, you close the gap between your vision and your reality.

This might feel impossible at first, but it's not. It's actually where you and others know you belong. In our research study, 94 percent of participants reported that someone had told them they have potential. More than 70 percent of participants also said there have been moments in their lives when they were living up to their full potential. People see something special in you, and deep down so do you.

People see something special in you, and deep down so do you.

Maybe you felt it with a new hobby. That first clay pot was a little lopsided, but you made it with your own hands and for a moment you had some undiscovered potential. Maybe it happened at work, when everything came together on a project and you got a tiny glimpse of what people call "being dialed in." Maybe it was in an exercise class that a friend dragged you to and you ended up loving. Maybe it was on a hike in Denali National Park where a glacier-sized thought hit you: "I was made for this!"

The Potential Zone looks different for every single person, but when you experience it, we all ask the same question: *How do I stay here?*

That's the question that inspired this entire project. Are there deliberate actions you can do that double, triple, quintuple your amount of time in the Potential Zone? Can you increase the number of best moments you experience? Are there steps you can take to change from being a tourist in the Potential Zone to a full-time resident?

There are, and I've seen thousands of people just like you do it. But it's not that easy because the Comfort Zone is so appealing.

I don't want to leave my Comfort Zone. Why would anyone want to? It's comfortable. There aren't many responsibilities. The expectations are low and easy to exceed. It requires nothing of you. You don't have to stretch, you don't have to grow, you don't have to ask for help or try anything that looks the tiniest bit challenging.

For decades I made my home in the Comfort Zone, but occasionally life would kick me out of it. My reality would shift so dramatically that I'd be propelled outside against my will. The pandemic certainly did that. I was comfortable in the reality that my company was positioned to have our best year in 2020. I'd spent the previous seven years working toward that moment, and in January 2020 I felt so confident about everything we had scheduled for the next twelve months. Guess what got canceled in 2020? Everything.

I was thrust outside my Comfort Zone whether I wanted to be or not. Left without many options, I had to learn how to do virtual events, launch a podcast, and teach online courses just to replace our revenue from live events. Am I thankful that now I have a podcast? Yep. Am I glad that now I know how to help people via online courses? Definitely. Did I willingly leave my Comfort Zone? No. I had to be dragged out, and I was furious. When I realized the largest part of my business had disappeared, I didn't immediately think, "What a wonderful opportunity to learn new skills that I might have otherwise missed! Change is fun!" Anyone who tells you they love change is either lying or a sociopath. Change sucks.

I hated being out of my Comfort Zone for the first nine months. (See previous confession of being a late bloomer to new ideas.) Eventually, when I realized the pandemic was not going to behave according to my personal time frame, I didn't have a choice. I had personally experienced one of the two reasons people leave their Comfort Zones:

1. Involuntary crisis
2. Voluntary trick

An involuntary crisis is when something disruptive happens outside of your control. You lose a job, fail in a relationship, have a health scare, or watch the rug get pulled out from under you. A crisis destroys your Comfort Zone. Sometimes the crisis isn't even yours. You might decide to leave the Comfort Zone because a friend or relative experienced a crisis and you want to avoid that same situation in your own life.

You might also voluntarily trick yourself out of the Comfort Zone. You get a glimpse of something you want more. Something in your life is missing and you quickly do the cost-benefit analysis. You decide the return on investment is worth the hard work of wooing yourself out of the Comfort Zone.

Except masochists, no one wants to leave their Comfort Zone. Why would you? It's delightful. You know the rules.

You know what to do. It's familiar. We've all had a friend date someone way below them. They've been engaged for seven years, he's been working on a business idea for five years while she supports him, and she's unhappy in the relationship. Why does she stay? Why do people stay at jobs they don't like? Why do any of us stay in situations we should have left long ago? Because they're comfortable. The Comfort Zone is not that exciting, but it's definitely a lot less scary than whatever is just over the border.

But maybe one day you get a little motivated. You attend an event, listen to a podcast, or find an encouraging social media account. (Those were three of the biggest sources of inspiration participants listed in the research study for this book.) You decide for a variety of reasons that seeing what you're capable of is worth it and quickly learn that it's not an easy endeavor. Convincing your stuck self to leave the Comfort Zone is like releasing a rehabilitated tiger into the wild. "Hey buddy, you don't have to live in that cage anymore. It's open. Just come on out and you can explore this entire jungle. It's all yours."

You often get mauled in the process, the tiger runs right back to the Comfort Zone, and you decide not to try again until New Year's rolls around once more and you get inspired with another resolution. I'm tired of that happening to both of us. It's enough already. But I also respect the Comfort Zone for the significant foe it is. It kicked my butt for decades. That's why we're going to proceed with caution and simplicity.

The caution is because we don't want to spook you deeper into the Comfort Zone. If you get even a hint that this is going to require years of work, focus, and persistence, you'll retire to an even harder to reach corner. Why wouldn't you? Who wants the promise of years of hard work, focus, and persistence, especially at the start of a new goal?

I love Malcolm Gladwell, but his explanation of K. Anders Ericsson's definition of expertise was discouraging to me. It takes ten thousand hours to become world-class? My full potential is ten thousand hours away?

Let's just do the math on that for a second. So, all I have to do is focus on my goal for ten hours a day and then I'll be an expert in three years? Do you have ten hours of free time each day that you've been looking to fill? Do you have seventy hours available this week for a new goal?

You're right, that's unrealistic. What if instead we just put in the work one hour a day? That's way more manageable. How long will that take to reach our potential?

Twenty-seven years.

If you have a free hour available for the next ten thousand days in a row—which, quite frankly, is going to be a challenge—you can tap into your potential in twenty-seven years. I'm currently forty-seven, which means at age seventy-four I'll really be coming into my own. That makes me young for Congress, and I'll probably be crushing a seniors' pickleball league at that point, but I don't want to wait that long for my potential.

You shouldn't either. If we come on too strong right out of the gate, that part of you that doesn't want to leave the Comfort Zone is going to smell a rat and bolt. So we're going to proceed with caution and also simplicity because the simpler the trick, the more likely you'll fall for it.

The Return of the Vision Wall

When you realize potential is just the gap between who you want to be and who you are right now, it's tempting to immediately ask, "What's the plan for my life?"

That's a reasonable question, but guess what wakes up when you ask it? The Vision Wall from chapter 1. It will present you with a terrible if-then offer: "If you can figure out what your plan is, then you can start working on your goal." What a perfect trap that is. Until you have a clear sense of your plan, your mission in life, you can't write one hundred words for a new book. Until you've reached the very core of your soul—your essence, if you will—you can't spend fifteen minutes walking around the neighborhood. Until you've identified your true north, your guiding star, your quest above all quests, you can't declutter this closet. *If* you'll do all of those things first, *then* you can get to work.

> **You'll quit before you start if the ticket price to trying is first understanding your vision.**

You'll quit before you start if the ticket price to trying is first understanding your vision. So put vision aside for a second. Let's start far simpler than that and just trick ourselves into answering one little question.

6

Pick the Big Game You Want to Win

Vision comes in a million varieties, which is why it's such a difficult thing to pick from, but there are really only five big games that all of life falls into:

1. Career
2. Finances
3. Relationships
4. Health
5. Fun

Every specific goal, task, or mission you can come up with will fit in one of those five big games. If you want to spend more time in the Potential Zone, start with one. All you have to do is answer the question, "What big game do I want to play?"

Here's how they break down.

Career

Want a promotion? Want to level up to senior executive vice president? Want to grow your freelance graphic design business? Want to build a makeup platform online as an influencer? Want to get more comfortable leading meetings at work? Play a career game.

Finances

Want to get out of debt? Want to retire comfortably? Want to buy a mountain or beach house? Want to pay for your kids' college? Want to figure out Bitcoin? Play a financial game.

Relationships

Want to repair a broken marriage? Want to get married? Want to be a better husband, dad, mother, son, or daughter? Did the pandemic make you realize, "Whoa, I need more friends because working from home is lonely"? Play a relationship game.

Health

Want to fit back into that pair of jeans? Want to feel better at the neighborhood pool? Want to finally sign up for a marathon? Want to lower your cholesterol? Want to improve how your knees feel? Want to do a better job managing your anxiety? Play a health game.

Fun

This is the final catch-all game. Anything that doesn't easily fit into the first four games lands here. Want to illustrate children's books? Want to learn how to knit? Want to read the whole Bible in a year? Want to train a

Belgian Malinois because you grew up with that kind of dog as a kid? Want to speak a new language? Play a fun game.

The helpful thing about this approach is that it immediately puts the stuck self at ease. If you ask, "What's your life mission?" you can hear the stuck self locking dead bolts on the other side of the Comfort Zone. But a game has a lot less pressure. It's just a game! It piques your sense of curiosity instead of rattling your fear of commitment. You don't even have to leave your Comfort Zone to answer the question, "What game do I want to play?"

The First Question

What big game do you want to play? That's the first question to address.

Pick one or two or all five if you've got the time.

When I started my blog, I could only play one game—a fun one. I didn't have time for any other games. I had a full-time job, two kids under the age of three, a beautiful wife, freelance clients, and an Atlanta commute. So I picked blogging and focused on that.

I'd run occasionally, but I didn't have a lot of free time to play a health game and train for half-marathons. I had friends, but I didn't have a lot of space for extra relationships outside of my family because my hours were so claimed. I worked faithfully for forty to forty-five hours each week at the office, but I didn't volunteer for a lot of extra projects because I wasn't playing a career game. (My blog would eventually lead to a new career, but I didn't know that at the beginning. It was just a fun game.)

Today, my life has a different shape. I have two teenage daughters. Saturdays, for instance, aren't spent trying desperately to keep toddlers entertained and alive from 6 a.m. to 8 p.m. L.E. is in college and spends her weekends on campus. McRae has cross-country and probably spent the night at a friend's house. If I want to work on a career game, a relationship game, and a fun game at the same time on a Saturday, I can because my commitments are different. That's not chaotic for me given my stage of life.

There are ways to increase the amount of time you have, but for the most part, accept the season you're in and play the number of games you can personally handle. Don't just admit the season you're in; give yourself credit for the games you're already playing and winning.

Eating dinner as a family is a game you might not be giving yourself enough credit for right now. Managing carpool for your kids is a game. Dealing with the new realities of a hybrid work schedule that's completely different from anything you've ever done is a game. If you can't fit a lot of new games in your schedule, it might not be because you're undisciplined. Chances are it's because you're already playing more games than you can even imagine.

If you're ready to play a new game, just pick your first one to get started. You don't even need a complicated creative exercise to brainstorm what goals you want to work on. If you tried your hand at a Best Moments List, you already have a sense of something you want more of. Even if you didn't, though, you already brought some goals to the table today. I know this because I've never met a single person who reads my books, takes my online courses, or listens to my podcast and says, "Jon, I don't have a single dream or plan."

High performers have dozens, hundreds, sometimes even thousands of things they want to do. Just pick one. You don't have to pick the right one—just pick the next one. Do it quickly. Let's get an easy win right away. There are only five choices. You can't even get it wrong because remember, you're the one making the rules in this game. If you pick fun, I'm not going to judge you and say, "You should have picked career." It's your game.

Don't worry about the steps you'll use to complete it either. In the next chapter, I'll show you the five specific ways to turn your game into an Easy Goal that anyone can accomplish. Right now, just put a little star by the game you're going to play. Then you can answer the second question.

The Second Question

If you're going to play a game and spend your most valuable resource—your time—on it, you should know the answer to the second question before you start: "What do I win?" That's the next question I want you to ask yourself.

Before you answer that, however, I need you to make me a promise: please be selfish and honest. False nobility won't get you out of the Comfort Zone. I see this with fellow authors all the time. When their books are about to launch they'll say, "If only one life is changed by my book, it was all worth it."

No it wasn't. That's not even a little true. Books are hard to write. The steps are simple but the work is challenging. It takes a thousand hours of wrestling with your ego, your expectations, and your fear that maybe @AngryDragonAllen287 on Twitter was right about how dumb you are. Books are too hard to write to help just one person. If that's your goal, spend thirty minutes writing a friend an email instead. That's way easier.

If you're going to go to all the trouble of writing a whole book, the win should be a lot bigger. You should want 100,000 people to buy it. You should want it to hit the *New York Times* Bestseller list. You should want it to make you lots of money. You should want strangers to stop you in the street and tell you how much your work changed their lives. You should want it to impact people around the world.

I've experienced all those things, and they're all really life-giving.

Writers say, "If only one life is changed by my book, it was all worth it" because we're afraid it won't sell and we're scared of looking selfish with our goal. Instead, we create fake desires that we think are socially acceptable and will shield us from future disappointment. We hedge our bets by lying about our expectations. If I tell myself selling only one copy is enough, then when it sells one hundred copies maybe I won't feel like a failure. But fake desires will never trick you out of a real Comfort Zone.

Fake desires will never trick you out of a real Comfort Zone.

False fuel won't give you the drive you need to stay in the Potential Zone. It's like putting diesel in a Ferrari and then wondering why it won't run.

So be selfish. If you've got some noble motivation about saving the world, awesome. Throw that in here, too, but don't hold back when you answer the question, "What do I win?"

Imagine you're in a negotiation with the part of you that's stuck in the Comfort Zone. There's another part of you that wants to change, so you call a meeting. Do you know the first and only question that stuck self is going to ask? "What's in it for me?"

If you work in sales for fourteen seconds, you quickly learn that's what everyone in the world is asking when it comes to making a decision.

What's in it for me?

Why should I do this?

What do I win if I do all this work?

If you come to the table with fake, boring wins, you'll get laughed right out of the room. Imagine trying to tell yourself, "If you work out, studies have shown your long-term chances of cardiovascular disease drop dramatically. Your bone density also really improves, so osteoporosis is much less of an issue later on in life."

That's not why I do CrossFit—a fact that's been so hard not to tell you until this far into the book. The first rule of CrossFit is that you have to constantly talk about CrossFit.

I would've never lifted a single, stupid kettlebell if that was my sales pitch to me. I don't love squats. Pull-ups stink. Don't get me started on weighted, one-arm sit-ups. Discipline didn't inspire me to stick with it. Willpower wasn't the deciding factor. Grit gave me nothing.

My stuck self is way smarter than that. He can see right through that phony character appeal to motivation. The only way to trick him out of the Comfort Zone is to convince him it's better out here than it is in there. He's not a bad guy. Let's not demonize any part of ourselves. He's part of who

I am, and I love who I am, but he's not motivated by logic or reason.

Humans are irrational. We're always doing things that don't make sense. I can't get my stuck self out of the Comfort Zone by using common sense. I can only lure him out patiently, and the best bait is a win. Even our stuck selves like how it feels to win. You might not consider yourself a competitive person, but given the choice between win and fail, you're picking win every time.

So I asked myself, "What do I win if I do CrossFit?" And then I came up with as many answers as I could.

1. The endorphins will make me feel better and will reduce stress.
2. Checking off the box on my chart after a workout will be really satisfying.
3. I will get to buy cool, new workout shoes.
4. I will like impressing my trainer with my consistency.
5. I will be able to create some new jokes I can use in speeches.
6. It will give me something to talk about with my friend Scott, who is into CrossFit.
7. I will feel more comfortable taking off my shirt at the neighborhood pool.

I logically know that if I stay in shape, I'll be around longer for my kids. I want that, clearly. But I'd be lying if I told you that on cold mornings when I don't want to exercise, I think to myself, "Remember, in eighteen years you'll be able to run around and keep up with your grandchildren who don't exist yet."

Most of the wins I listed weren't noble. A few were even vain. But that's OK because my only goal initially is to get my stuck self out of the Comfort Zone.

The long-term benefits of your goal will change your life, your family, and maybe even your community. One of the natural by-products of living in your full potential is that you want to help other people live in theirs too. This journey starts with self but ends in service. That's wonderful, but very few people will leave a Comfort Zone for that reason alone. On the flip side, helping a community of people is one of the greatest reasons you'll stay in the Potential Zone.

This journey starts with self but ends in service.

You don't have to come up with seven wins like my list for CrossFit. I'm a writer and we're wordy! But write down a few. You picked up this book for a reason. There's something about your life you want to change. Which game does it fall into, and if you play it, what do you win?

If you do a little work, if you take a step or two to close the gap between your vision and your reality, what's in it for you?

This will feel counterintuitive at first because most of the time when we begin new goals we start with the work, not the reward. We brainstorm all the actions we'll need to do to accomplish the goal. That's an important step, and we'll do that next but not first. Why? Because it's overwhelming. If you feel stuck and the first thing you do is come up with a massive list of all the work you'll have to do to get unstuck, do you think you feel more motivated or less?

First dream about the win, and then we can decide about the work.

The Third Question

We're not out of the Comfort Zone yet, but we've piqued the interest of our stuck selves a little with a few possible wins. We've pushed a ladder against the wall and are peeking out over the top with more curiosity than we've felt in years.

We might even be ready for our third question: *How do I win?*

If the new best moment is worth it, this is naturally the next question you ask when it comes to playing a new game. That best moment you just described sounds good, and you're thinking, *I like good things. How do I get that good thing? How do I use more of my potential?*

Now for the best idea in the entire book . . . the answer is, you win the game by making the game easy.

Did that feel as wrong as picking wins that initially seem selfish on the surface? Be honest, I bet it did. But if you've tried what you're supposed to do when you want to achieve goals and it hasn't worked, it might be time to try something counterintuitive, like playing an easier game. The best way to escape the Comfort Zone is to make the wins big and the work small.

I initially felt a little uncomfortable even suggesting this until I started to study highly successful people. The executions are all different, but they all share similar elements when it comes to performance. One of these is that they always make their games easy to win. They are obsessed with setting themselves up for success. Marshall Goldsmith, an executive coach who's been labeled the world's number one leadership thinker and sold millions of books, admitted as much in his classic *What Got You Here Won't Get You There*. He writes, "I make it easy on myself. I don't place sucker bets. I only work with clients who have an extremely high potential of succeeding. Why would anyone want to operate any other way?"[1]

He's not the only one who does that. After spending decades in the trenches of some of the most accomplished companies in the world, Goldsmith has noticed something consistent about high achievers: "As you go through life, contemplating the mechanics of success and wondering why some people are successful and others are not, you'll find that this is one of the defining traits of habitual winners. They stack the deck in their favor. And they're unabashed about it."[2]

Most people do just the opposite of making things easier. They make up rules for their goals that guarantee they'll lose.

I first ran into this reality while doing the research for my book *Finish*. Dr. Mike Peasley and I studied nearly nine hundred people for six months as they worked on their goals. Midway through the project we realized that most participants overestimated what they could accomplish and unconsciously created impossible games. Instead of stacking the deck in their favor, they had come up with wildly difficult goals at the outset and then almost immediately ran into the frustrating constraints of reality. In essence, they set a massive vision that was completely divorced from reality and were dying in the gap between the two.

To address that problem, we encouraged them to cut their goals in half and were surprised at what happened. People who took this unusual approach were 63 percent more successful.

When I send that idea to clients in my slide deck before an event, they always call me up and say, "Will you please remove that terrible idea that tells our sales team to sell half as many products this year?" But that idea isn't prescriptive. The way to succeed isn't to set a false vision at the beginning and then cut it in half in the middle of the project. That stat is just indicative of how tempting it is at the beginning of a goal to set ourselves up for failure by playing unnecessarily difficult games.

This happens primarily for three reasons:

1. Deliberate self-sabotage

If you make the rules and expectations impossible, you can fail quickly and blame the rules and the expectations, not yourself. Gay Hendricks, author of *The Big Leap*, calls this an Upper Limit problem. People often set limits on what's an acceptable amount of success, afraid that they'll outshine a family member or abandon their humbler roots or that they flat-out don't deserve to be happy. When they approach their Upper Limit, they unknowingly pull back in the form of self-sabotage.[3]

2. A lack of self-awareness

It's hard to create rules that will help you win if you don't know yourself a little bit. If I'm a morning person but I've never stopped to notice that, I might end up putting too many important work tasks late in the afternoon when I'm at my creative worst. A rule like "Do the hardest work first thing in the morning" would serve me well, but if I don't know what makes me tick, I'll never create it and miss all the benefits of making my day easier. That's part of the reason that making a Best Moments List is so helpful. It introduces you to you.

3. A sense of guilt

If our unspoken rule is "Goals must be difficult to count," when we create an easy one for ourselves it feels like cheating. It's not "hard enough," and instead we write rigid rules until the game gets so challenging that our stuck self decides the change isn't worth it.

This book will definitely help you with self-awareness, but if you'd like to explore the origin of self-sabotage and a sense of guilt with a counselor, then by all means do so. That's not my mission today.

I want us to set such a low bar that it's impossible for us to fail and we get a quick win that encourages us to keep trying. The faster we win the game, the quicker we'll commit to the work. The more often we win, the more often we'll try.

When you get a few quick wins, you'll discover a secret about the Comfort Zone: it's not that wide.

You don't have to slog through the Comfort Zone for months to escape. The Comfort Zone is tall but skinny. It looks intimidating to get over but only takes a few minutes to get through. The first drop of sweat, the first hundred words of your book, the first few cold calls to clients—all of your quick wins make the Comfort Zone evaporate.

How do we make sure we get some? We build an Easy Goal.

7

Escape the Comfort Zone with an Easy Goal

I had 1,132 ideas in 2021.

I don't mean that I had "like a ton of ideas" in 2021. I mean I had exactly 1,132. I know that because I kept a running numerical list of them for a solid year in a series of notebooks.

I don't believe in writer's block. I believe in idea bankruptcy. If you can't sit down to write something, it just means your idea vault is empty. If I want to be better writer, I need to be a better thinker, which means I need more ideas. I turned that hope into a goal, and every year I get a little better at it. I had 1,563 ideas in 2022.

In June 2020, I took vitamins 28 out of 30 days.

In October of that same year, I made the bed first thing in the morning 26 out of 31 days.

Two months ago, I walked up the stairs 28 days in a row. I'm high energy and tend to sprint up any staircase like an eight-year-old trying to hide from bedtime. At some point I'm going to trip and break something, so I decided to change that habit.

Last month I overlooked an offense for 27 out of 30 days. I found myself being offended at the dumbest things, so I measured whether I could fix that.

When I say I'm a goal nerd, I'm not exaggerating. I've tried hundreds of different types of goals and helped thousands of people with thousands more. In all those years, I've found that there are three types of goals that are the most productive for tapping into your full potential:

1. Easy Goals
2. Middle Goals
3. Guaranteed Goals

They're similar in some regards, but what they accomplish is different.

Easy Goals help you escape the Comfort Zone.

Middle Goals help you avoid the Chaos Zone.

Guaranteed Goals help you live in the Potential Zone.

Nearly everyone I know wants to start with Guaranteed Goals because they're the most ambitious. "Go big or go home" is a fun phrase to say, but that sentiment has also sent more people back to the Comfort Zone than any other terrible Instagram mantra. In some specific situations, such an aggressive approach to goals actually sends people back to the hospital.

Erin Quillman, an occupational therapy assistant in Detroit, told me that she often "has to tell people to slow down so they

EASY GOALS
help you escape
the Comfort Zone.

MIDDLE GOALS
help you avoid
the Chaos Zone.

GUARANTEED GOALS
help you live
in the Potential Zone.

don't hurt themselves further or reinjure themselves. They feel better, their pain is masked sometimes, and they have some strength but can really do damage if they progress too hard or too fast." If you're an occupational therapist, your whole world revolves around creating smaller goals today to help people reach bigger goals tomorrow.

There is a tiny fraction of people who can go from couch to Ironman, from writing zero books to a complete trilogy, from messy house to "I have a distinct purpose for every pair of socks I own." But for the rest of us mere mortals, the greatest path to long-term success always starts with Easy Goals that turn into Middle Goals and eventually grow into Guaranteed Goals.

Think of it like a goal ladder with three rungs. One of the vertical rails is effort and the other rail is time. The higher you climb, from Easy to Middle to Guaranteed, the greater amounts of effort and time you need to accomplish the goal. Easy Goals are at the bottom. They're simple to reach and you barely have to take your foot off the ground. At the top of the ladder are Guaranteed Goals, which take a significant investment. In the middle are—get ready to have your mind blown—Middle Goals.

Take out the big game you picked to play (career, finances, relationships, health, or fun) and start at the bottom of the ladder. Create an Easy Goal that has the following five characteristics.

1. Easy Goals have short time frames.

An Easy Goal can be accomplished in one to seven days. If it takes you a month, it's not an Easy Goal.

For example, when I realized I had plateaued in a few areas of my business, I came up with an Easy Goal. All I had to do was ask Brad Lomenick, the most networked person I've ever met, for the name of a business coach he'd recommend. That goal took a fifteen-minute conversation on a Tuesday in Atlanta backstage at an event. Once I had accomplished that and enjoyed the quick win, my next Easy Goal was to write an email to the person Brad suggested. I wrote a 108-word email and asked the coach if we could set up a thirty-minute call. I then had the call. Three Easy Goals that I could accomplish in a week. I didn't reinvent my business; that would have sent my stuck self right back into the Comfort Zone. Instead, I said, "Hey, let's just try this for a week and see what happens." I might repeat an Easy Goal for a few weeks in a row, but I'm only thinking about it in seven-day chunks at most.

A short time frame also disrupts the fear that if you try something once, you have to do it forever. Perfectionists especially will resist attempting new goals because it feels like a lifelong commitment. "Winners never quit!" we mistakenly think. But an Easy Goal is the opposite. An Easy Goal is speed dating, not a marriage. You've got a scheduled "out" after a day or a week if you decide the goal isn't right for you.

2. Easy Goals have obvious first steps.

If there's the slightest confusion at the start of your goal, your stuck self will cry, "Foul!" With an Easy

Goal, you can always figure out "the Next Right Thing," to borrow a phrase from author Emily P. Freeman.

Learning CrossFit wasn't complicated at first. My neighbor Caleb Gregory owns CrossFit East Nashville, one of the most popular gyms in town. I told him I was interested in training (first step). I got his phone number (second step). I texted him and set up a time to meet (third step). I went to his house, where he has that dungeon type of garage every CrossFitter has, and did a simple assessment with him (fourth step). I took notes on our conversation and put them into a simple chart in Microsoft Word where I could track my progress (fifth step). Please note that at this point I hadn't even done CrossFit yet, but the first five steps were obvious, and I could do them in a week—Easy Goal.

3. Easy Goals are not expensive.

Have you ever purchased something expensive because you thought you needed it for a new goal? You bought the type of compound bow professional hunters use on bull elk before even shooting a single arrow. You got mildly interested in making your own sushi and picked up a $500 Sakai Takayuki 33-Layer Damascus Gingami No. 3 used by the top chefs in the world. You were invited to go cycling by some guys in the neighborhood and purchased a racing bike that cost more than your first car.

That last one hits close to home—specifically, my garage wall—because that's where the bike I barely rode hung. I broke rule number 3, "Easy Goals are not expensive," and decided to overinvest right at the beginning of my cycling adventure. Instead of borrowing a bike from my good friend Dean, who has a veritable fleet, I went all in and paid for what would become a carbon fiber monument to impulse buys. I felt ashamed every time I walked by it in the garage because I spent so much money on that bike and wasn't using it.

If your initial goal costs a lot of money to accomplish, you've just given your stuck self an amazing excuse not to do it. I didn't hire a business coach as part of my Easy Goal. That would come much later. I didn't sign up for a year-long membership to a CrossFit gym right out of the gate. When I started my blog all those years ago, I used Blogspot, a free service. I hosted it the cheapest way possible and built it myself (poorly, I might add). Eighteen months in, I paid a designer $3,000 to build a real website, but if I had made the initial goal expensive, I never would have tried. An Easy Goal always starts out cheap. There's so much emotional baggage related to money. Don't add it to the mix when you're just getting started.

4. **Easy Goals match your current schedule.**
At the start of new goals, we tend to make big sweeping declarations that are completely divorced from reality and then act surprised when they don't work. I'll show you how to remix reality a bit when we get to your Guaranteed Goals, but an Easy Goal should match your current reality. I didn't quit my job when

I first started blogging. That's dramatic and maybe makes for a good story on Instagram: "I moved to Paraguay with only nine dollars and a pencil!" But that's not what I did. To start my blog, I just found thirty minutes a few times a week when I could write. That was easy. Committing to go to the gym five times this week when your current schedule only accommodates one time may sound heroic, but you're setting yourself up for automatic failure. An Easy Goal doesn't require you to overhaul your entire reality to accomplish it. At most, it should take around 1 percent of your time in a week, which is less than two hours. You get it in where you can fit it in. (If you're married, Easy Goals are also a lot easier for spouses to support at the beginning than the massive plans we often tell them about.)

5. Easy Goals feel like they're "not enough."
Do you know what a high performer who's been stirred out of the Comfort Zone always wants? MORE! After doing weekly Easy Goals with CrossFit, I told my trainer Caleb, "I don't feel like I'm doing enough."

He asked, "Would you like to overdo it in these first few weeks and then never do it again?"

I laughed and said, "Yeah, that's kind of my MO."

"That's what I thought," said Caleb. "That's why we're building a foundation."

Easy Goals build small structures. They wake up muscle memory. They give you that first bit of momentum. If you feel like you're not doing enough yet, that's a good sign. Jeffery J. Downs and Jami L. Downs wrote the book on consistency—literally. *Streaking* teaches you how to accomplish massive goals in tiny ways. One of their rules is that the Easy Goal you decide to streak should be so simple it's laughable. When you share it with friends, their response should be, "Is that all?" Jami says, "If the activity sounds impressive when said aloud, it is probably too hard."[1]

Use those five factors like a filter to see if your goal is easy enough.

If it takes ninety days to accomplish, it's not easy.

If you can't figure out what to do first, make it smaller.

If it stretches you financially, find a cheaper way to do it.

If it requires you to be an entirely new person with a radically different schedule to complete it, go back to the drawing board.

If friends are amazed when you tell them about it, listen to Jami—it's too hard.

Easy Goals make escaping from the Comfort Zone . . . easy.

They'll also provide additional insight into what you really care about. If you can't get excited about an Easy Goal that takes less than two hours, costs next to nothing, and lasts a week, no wonder you gave up on it when you made it a New Year's resolution. If it couldn't hold your attention for a week, of course it wasn't the right goal for a whole year. That's why when the fitness app Strava analyzed 31.5 million activities, they could identify the second Friday in January as "Quitter's Day." More people gave up on their goals on that day than any other.

One week, I tried three different Easy Goals:

1. Complain less often
2. Criticize less often
3. Network with more people

The first week I attempted these goals, I wrote down my results on four of the days. So I tried it for another week. The second week I didn't measure those goals at all. I went 0 for 7. The same thing happened the third and fourth weeks. Despite my best efforts, I couldn't get into these goals. Even at the easiest level, I wasn't willing to put in the work.

I quit all three with zero shame. If the only rung I had on my goal ladder was "New Year's resolution," I would've felt like a failure for the rest of the year. Instead, I was able to say, "I tried those Easy Goals and didn't care about them. Next!" An Easy Goal makes it easy to quit goals you shouldn't have tried in the first place.

How long should you work on your Easy Goals? I can't give you an exact answer. I focused on Easy Goals for sixteen weeks with CrossFit before I transitioned to Middle Goals. I only did Easy Goals with my writing for a few weeks before I leveled up my effort. It really depends on how stuck you are in the game you're playing and what you want to accomplish. What I can tell you is what's going to happen next.

You'll sprint right out of the Comfort Zone, through the Potential Zone, and wind up smack-dab in the middle of the Chaos Zone. How do I know?

Because you're a rabbit too.

8

Skip the Chaos Zone with a Middle Goal

The most famous story about wasted potential is "The Tortoise and the Hare." If it's been years since you've read this fable, allow me to summarize it.

An arrogant rabbit makes fun of a turtle for being slow. In response, the turtle challenges the rabbit to a race. The rabbit jumps out to a quick lead and decides to show the turtle how fast he really is by taking a nap on the side of the road. What a perfect picture of making a goal harder than it needs to be. If the rabbit were to keep running, even at 10 percent speed, he could win easily.

The turtle passes the sleeping rabbit, and despite the rabbit's frantic sprint when he finds out what happened, the turtle wins the race. Though this phrase doesn't appear in Aesop's original text, the moral of the story is, "Slow and steady wins the race." The turtle is the picture of full potential. He runs his race. He doesn't nap. He doesn't sprint. He just stays faithful and eventually wins.

That story discouraged me the first time I heard it as a kid. I didn't want to be a turtle, plodding slowly toward victory like a rock with legs. I wanted to run! I felt like a rabbit in a world built for turtles. No wonder it was so hard for me tap into my full potential. If turtles are the picture of success but you're by nature a rabbit, you're screwed.

Curse this turtle-filled planet! I'm not a rabbit—I'm a victim! The system is stacked against me. How can I possibly tap into my full potential when it means I have to become the opposite of me?

I was doomed by my inconsistency.

I'm not naturally good at applying consistent effort over time to a specific goal. My youngest daughter once said to me, "Dad, you're either OCD or NoCD," meaning either I was hyperfocused or I was completely aloof. I have two speeds: neutral or nitro.

I got a 2.4 GPA my first semester of college, was on the verge of losing all my scholarships, and then sprinted my way to a 4.0 the second semester to save the day. That was the hardest possible way to get a B average for the year. I then repeated that same, stressful experience several times before I graduated, rabbiting my way to a diploma.

Twelve years later, I started to break this all-or-nothing habit, but it wasn't because I matured or grew wiser. When my blog started to grow, I couldn't help but notice all the wins I got when I was consistent. I didn't have to hit home runs with my content every day. Even average, consistent content beats amazing, inconsistent content. If you don't have quality first—and no one does when you start something new—consistency will carry you. This works because of a simple principle about time and performance: *everything you apply time to gets better.*

The more hours you spend exercising than last month, the better shape you'll be in this month.

> **Everything you apply time to gets better.**

The more hours you spend with your kids, the better you'll know them.

The more hours you spend serving clients, the more business you'll get.

The more hours you spend reading, the more new ideas you'll have.

The more hours you spend applying to jobs, going on interviews, and networking, the more likely you are to get hired.

Other than destructive activities—like, say, drinking, smoking, or rollerblading—it's hard to think of a game in your life where this principle doesn't work.

The turtle doesn't beat the rabbit in the race because he is faster. The turtle beats the rabbit because he has a middle gear and the rabbit doesn't. The rabbit has only two gears: sprint or sleep. The race starts, he takes off, and immediately he is destroying the tortoise. As the story says, "The hare was soon out of sight."

When you step out of your Comfort Zone and experience an Easy Goal, you will be tempted to run "soon out of sight" right into the Chaos Zone.

Your friends and family members won't even know what just happened because suddenly you're sprinting. You're not just eating healthier, you're doing Whole30 and editing your entire fridge with a vengeance. You're bringing your own meals in Tupperware to friends' houses because you're not sure if they completely respect your approach to macros. You went from doing nothing to doing everything, and it gives everyone around you whiplash.

This is a completely natural process and nothing to be ashamed of. It happens because we think to ourselves, "If an Easy Goal felt good, a massive goal would feel a hundred times better." Like the monkey who figures out pressing a button drops a food pellet, we start hitting that button faster and faster. We kick our lives into the only other gear we've known before—the sprint gear. That's how we end up in the Chaos Zone without even noticing what was happening.

Wait a second, did we just run by the Potential Zone? Did we jump right from Comfort to Chaos? We did. That's why it's called a yo-yo diet—binge or purge, feast or famine. When you've got only two gears, you end up only two places: the Comfort Zone or the Chaos Zone. But in the middle of those two extremes is where the real fun happens. That's the Potential Zone, and to get there we need Middle Goals.

Middle Goals

The best part about the Potential Zone is that it's huge. Imagine a line that goes from 0 to 100. Zero is the Comfort Zone and 100 is the Chaos Zone. Guess what 1–99 is? The Potential Zone. More than none is 1; less than 100 is 99. Everything in between is the Potential Zone. You don't have to be precise or perfect to stay in the Potential Zone. You just have to consistently try. In a marathon, the starting line is two feet wide, the finish line is two feet wide, and the other 138,431 feet is the middle of the race.

A good Middle Goal takes the mystery out of consistency and gives you five clear signs you're on the right track.

1. **Middle Goals have time frames of thirty to ninety days.**

   It takes me thirty days to do twenty CrossFit workouts. That's not an Easy Goal for me. Twenty different times on twenty different days, I have to find a free hour in my busy schedule. I'm willing to do that because all the wins I enjoyed during my Easy Goals told me I was capable of that.

   If you can accomplish the goal in a long weekend, it's not a Middle Goal. If it takes you six months to finish it, it's not a Middle Goal. The time frame is your quickest clue that you've built a good Middle Goal.

2. **Middle Goals are flexible.**

   We're using Middle Goals to develop consistency, so it's important that we have a wide variety of ways we can work on them. I think about it like having a really large Swiss Army knife. If you have only one blade— "Run on my favorite trail," "Write for three hours," or "Quietly work on my business plan in my home office"—you'll rarely make progress. But every action you add to your goal is like adding another tool to a Swiss Army knife so you're always prepared.

   If I'm full of energy and have a few free hours in my morning, I'm excited to write. But if I'm on a plane and

I'm tired, I'll listen to an audiobook instead. If I'm even too exhausted for that, I'll watch a documentary on the topic I'm writing about. If I'm somewhere in between high and low energy, I'll edit pages I've already written. I have a list of twenty-five different actions that count toward my goal of writing. That's like having twenty-five tools on my Swiss Army knife. I'm ready for any amount of time, location, or energy level when it comes to moving my goal forward. The way you do that is by being flexible and having dozens of actions at your disposal when you find a little bit of time in your schedule. Watching a documentary, doing ten push-ups, or spending fifteen minutes decluttering a room might not feel like much, but an inch forward is a mile of progress to someone who never moved.

3. **Middle Goals don't fall apart if you miss a day.** We're aiming for consistency, not perfection. You're going to miss a few days. There's a big chance you won't go 30 for 30 or 90 for 90. The benefit of a Middle Goal is that it's a long enough time frame that you've got a chance to catch up.

A friend of mine approached her step goals that way. Her Middle Goal was to walk 10,000 steps every day. That's a lot of steps in a month! But she quickly realized that there were some days when it was impossible. With schedule conflicts she might get only 2,000 steps in, feel like a failure, and then quit the whole goal. She decided to change the rules. Now she shoots for 70,000 steps in a week. That way, if she misses her goal on a Tuesday, she gives herself the weekend to catch up.

If a streak goal works for you, awesome. Use it. If it doesn't, give yourself a chance to catch up. A good Middle Goal is never so rigid that it becomes fragile.

4. Middle Goals encourage you to tweak your schedule.
You barely have to touch your schedule to accomplish an Easy Goal, but a Middle Goal requires a little more intentionality. Can you find 3 percent of your week to work on your goal? That's roughly five hours.

I know it sounds like I carry a stopwatch around with me and I'm constantly saying, "I would like to use 2.3 minutes on this activity," but I promise I'm not that precise. I just think it's helpful to put our time into context.

If I tell you that I'm too busy to turn an Easy Goal into a Middle Goal, what I'm saying is, "I'm too busy to find 3 percent of my week. Yes, I'm desperate to change my life, but I simply can't change 3 percent of my week." If you're a leader and one of your employees refuses to make a 3 percent change in their performance, you know instantly that they aren't very serious about their career.

5. Middle Goals have patience built in.
I'm not a patient person. I wear out the elevator button, believing that the more times I press it, the faster it will get to me. I refuse to watch YouTube videos that show me five-second ads before they start. A microwave has never reached zero in my presence. "It's close enough!" I declare, stirring around chunks of ice in

whatever I pulled out too early. I abhor patience, but anything of substance requires it.

With a Middle Goal, patience is automatic because you can't binge-hustle it. A Middle Goal should take you thirty days to finish. If your Middle Goal is to take vitamins for thirty days, guess what you can't do on the last day of the month? Take thirty vitamins all at once. A good Middle Goal has pace built in because it can't be accomplished overnight. It must be focused on over time, day by day. You can catch up on days you missed, but you can't accomplish the whole thing in a mad dash.

What Middle Goals should you try? Well, what Easy Goal did you love? I loved tracking my writing hours for a week. With just a short game, I could tell that might be fun to try for a whole month.

Not every Easy Goal will graduate to a Middle Goal. On average, only about 20 percent of the Easy Goals I try make it all the way to the top of the ladder and become Guaranteed Goals. For example, I tested whether I could take collagen in my morning coffee every day for a week. Then I tried it for a month, and then finally for a year. As I write this, I have a small packet of it with me for a trip to San Antonio. (It's for my knees, not my lips, which if anything are already too plump.) That one turned into a Middle Goal, but another knee-related Easy Goal didn't.

I once tried to take one hundred backward steps every day because a knee expert said it was good for you. It probably is, but I didn't enjoy it, and I looked like a weirdo doing it in my neighborhood. I retired that Easy Goal after only four days. No need to middle that one.

During the research process for this book, we took thousands of people through goal-setting challenges. One of the core principles we tested were Middle Goals. Instead of trying to write a whole book, lose a hundred pounds, start a company, or anything on the chaos scale of things, we focused on Middle Goals. I encouraged participants to choose three fifteen-minute actions and stay faithful to them over a period of ninety days. There was a chart with a checklist, video content from me, and daily text reminders. I made the game as easy as possible for everyone.

Nobody really liked that at first. Everyone wanted to sprint. I could tell when I taught this lesson on day 1 that there was a general sense of "Is that all?" Turtles never sign up for goal-setting research projects, only rabbits do. But after the ninety days, the results revealed that Middle Goals work.

Of those surveyed, 92 percent reported that they tapped into more of their potential. That's a fun number, but the one I liked even more was this: 88 percent of people said when they focused on their small actions, it helped them think about bigger goals too. Consistency is contagious. When you practice it in small, easy ways, it impacts you in big ways on other goals.

Angela Belford picked "build my platform" as her Middle Goal. That's a really popular choice right now because the internet offers us all the opportunity to build an audience that supports a business. Angela shared her middle results with me:

(1) I completed my four-week journal that's a lead generator for my email list. (2) I launched my podcast. My fifth episode posted yesterday. (3) I launched my first five-day online challenge.

Consistency is contagious.

Those are all new accomplishments, but what was interesting is that the Middle Goal woke up an old goal too. Angela said, "I wrote my book *Be Freaking Awesome* in 2017 but have done zero to promote it since 2018." Her stuck self kept that book on a shelf. But when she learned how to live in the Potential Zone, she says, "I literally did more in the last ninety days than I did in three years. Woo-freaking-hoo!!!"

Do you know how fun it is when you revive an old goal and actually see results? Angela does.

Kate Homonai experienced the same type of results but decided to share her feedback in the form of a fake complaint. She wrote, "I would like to lodge a non-complaint about the unproblematic side effects of this challenge." What were her two "issues"?

(1) It has become too easy for me to walk a mile. I don't get any active minute points on my tracker because walking a mile does almost nothing to my heart rate anymore. (2) My day runs too smoothly when I set aside ten minutes to plan. I don't forget things or feel overwhelmed. Is this what it feels like to be responsible and on top of things?

Middle Goals are magic, and small consistent actions always turn into an even bigger best moment. Monica Lamb picked three goals and they all grew:

(1) "Get up at a specific time every day" turned into getting up and having a plan. (2) "Walk a mile every day" grew into two to three miles, daily tracking my steps, tracking my food, and losing ten pounds. (3) "Spend fifteen minutes on your platform" has become a brand-new mission-focused ministry.

That's what's so fun about Middle Goals—they have the potential to grow. If Monica's Middle Goal had been "Walk three miles every day," she would've been discouraged by the size of it and quit. That's Chaos Zone behavior, going from zero miles a day to three. Instead, she chose the middle, set the goal as one mile, discovered the Potential Zone, and grew her goal to two to three miles every day, tracking steps, tracking food, and losing ten pounds.

Maybe Monica will go on to lose twenty pounds. Maybe she'll walk five miles a day. Maybe she'll run a half-marathon. Once you've tapped into your Potential Zone, any dream feels possible. Monica can easily turn any of her Middle Goals into even bigger Guaranteed Goals if she wants to, and so can you.

Renee Mildbrandt made her game successful by creating a great Middle Goal: "100 words is enough." She used to play a harder game where she told herself, "If you can't write 1,000 words a day, don't bother." That's a much more impressive-sounding goal, but the reality is she wrote zero words when that was her approach because that was a Chaos Zone goal. We always hold ourselves to impossible standards in the Chaos Zone.

At first, I bet consistently writing 100 words a day didn't feel like what a "real writer" would do, but the letter Renee wrote me proved it was working: "I'm currently at 74,002 words," she said, "and I'll be finished writing my book by the end of the month." She Middle-Goaled her way to an entire book.

Participant after participant, page after page, those were the stories I kept hearing. The reason isn't surprising.

When you avoid the Chaos Zone with a Middle Goal, you don't burn out and give up. You end up playing whatever game you picked more often. When you play more often, you win more often. When you win more often, you play more often. It's cyclical.

It all sounds so easy, right? In the immortal words of ousted GE CEO Jeff Immelt, responding to critics who attacked him with their suggestions of what they would've done in his position, "Every job looks easy when you're not the one doing it."[1] Let's not beat around the bush or sugarcoat the hard work that success always requires.

When you play more often, you win more often. When you win more often, you play more often.

Middle Goals are more challenging than Easy Goals, hence the name. As a rule, they cost more of your most limited resource, the one thing you can never get more of—time. No one has ever had enough time. I'm sure cave dwellers were always complaining that between woolly mammoth hunting, wall painting, and sabertooth tiger avoiding, it was impossible to find some "me time."

Nobody has ever had it easy when it comes to time management, but it's harder for you because, unlike a cave dweller, you carry a casino in your pocket.

9

Plan a Calendar Heist

Potential is hard because Netflix is easy.

Potential is hard because Instagram is easy.

Potential is hard because Facebook is easy.

You might not often think about companies like that in the same sentence as your own potential, but you should.

Twitter doesn't want you to start a business. TikTok doesn't want you to run a half-marathon. HBO Max doesn't want you to write a book. Even dating apps don't want you to have a long, healthy marriage. They want you to have a hundred meaningless dates because then you'll never end your paid subscription to their service.

Whenever you dare to spend more time exploring your potential and less time distracted, hundreds of thousands of people get very nervous. It's true. The modern world is designed to keep you from living up to your full potential.

Do you know the goal of every single one of the 58,456 employees at Facebook? To distract you. They're not trying to connect you with old friends from high school. They don't care that you love chinchillas and finally found a group of other people in the Twin Cities who love them too. They're not trying to educate you about the news. They're trying to turn your attention into ad revenue. And they should be! They're an attention-based business. There are entire companies whose entire business model is your time. So if you're finding it difficult to make time for Middle Goals, don't beat yourself up. The odds are stacked against you.

There are entire companies whose entire business model is your time.

Why did this happen? Why is it harder for you to tap into your full potential now? Because distraction technology scaled faster than our ability to focus. Can you even begin to imagine the strides we've made in distraction technology in the last twenty years?

The main distraction I had on the first cell phone I owned was a game called *Snake*. Remember that one? If you're my age, you just smiled a little bit. It was a 2-bit, black-and-white game where a line slowly scrolled across the screen. Riveting.

That was the only distraction on my phone.

Now my phone contains every known form of entertainment ever created. It contains thousands and thousands of video games. It contains thousands and thousands of podcasts. It contains millions of books. It contains access to the more than five hundred hours of video content that is uploaded to YouTube every minute. My phone contains the latest and most dynamic social media sites, instantly connecting me to anyone I've ever met, gone to school with, or seen in one of those movies it also contains. I can comment on The Rock's Instagram posts!

And other than perhaps the calculator, every single app on our phones is trying to sell us something.

You have a casino in your pocket. This is less of a metaphor and more of a reality because software designers use "persuasive design" to create apps with techniques first perfected in the casino industry. Oliver Burkeman makes note of this in his book *Four Thousand Weeks: Time Management for Mortals*:

> One example among hundreds is the ubiquitous drag-down-to-refresh gesture, which keeps people scrolling by exploiting a phenomenon known as "variable rewards": when you can't predict whether or not refreshing the screen will bring new posts to read, the uncertainty makes you more likely to keep trying, again and again and again, just as you would on a slot machine.[1]

No wonder it's so easy to get lost on our phones. I knew I was doomed when I witnessed something on that family vacation to Costa Rica I mentioned earlier. We were staying in an amazing cliffside hotel that had a huge infinity pool overlooking the Pacific Ocean. Every evening the sun would glide into the end of the day like a painting falling off a wall. There were even a pair of colorful macaws that would fly across the vista as if they'd been released by an animal handler. It was ridiculous.

One night, as I was watching the sunset, I noticed that the twenty people around me were all on their phones. There wasn't a single person watching the sunset. I knew in that moment, if the phone is going to whup a Costa Rican ocean sunset, of course it's going to win against something challenging.

If this vista is going to lose to this device, how in the world can I expect to focus on a Tuesday when I'm in my office?

Have you ever thought about that? Your distractions get louder the more you focus on goals that are difficult. I'm never distracted when I'm binge-watching Netflix. I'm never distracted when I'm scrolling through Instagram. I'm never distracted when I'm running down rabbit holes on YouTube. (Has anyone in the history of the internet only watched one video on YouTube?) I have a pretty easy time focusing in those moments. I only have a hard time focusing when it comes to things that matter.

The odds are stacked against you when it comes to your potential, but the house doesn't have to win this game. You don't need a new time management system or approach to productivity. You'll never beat a casino that way. The only way you'll come out on top is with a four-letter question.

The Reason Your To-Do List Is Never Finished

Most goals are optimistic lies. I hate to step on so many toes, but it's true.

We believe we'll do them, though, and we declare our intentions with gusto.

We will run!

We will write our book!

We will build a business, lose the weight, eat better, sleep more, and a thousand other noble things! We will tap into our massive potential!

I once had a counselor tell me that's called living in "verbal reality," which is the belief that just saying something makes it true. It's a telltale sign that you're not living in the Potential Zone.

My favorite example of this is how I used to pack for vacation. I love to read. When we'd go on a seven-day trip, I would pack seven books, kind of like underwear—one for each day. My suitcase would weigh a thousand pounds as I dragged this mini library through the airport.

During the trip, I'd read half of one book. I'd export seven books to the beach, show them the Gulf of Mexico, and then import them back into my house. *Wasn't that a fun trip, guys? I sure enjoyed carrying you eight hundred miles and not cracking 90 percent of you open once.*

Before we left for the trip, I was convinced I would read every one of those books. I couldn't imagine not having those books with me. I told a small but physically heavy, optimistic lie. Why was it a lie? Because I've never read a 300-page business book in a single day, never mind seven in seven days. Who was this speed-reader I imagined I'd become on vacation?

I wasn't going to be reading six hours a day for the next seven days. I was going to abandon the books as soon as my kids wanted to throw a Frisbee on the beach or my wife wanted to take a walk. My goal—the amount of reading I planned— was completely disconnected from the reality of my calendar and was thus an optimistic lie.

To start addressing that, all I had to do was answer one question: *When?*

That's the first question I always ask somebody when they tell me about a goal they want to do.

When?

I don't care about the why at first.

I don't care about the how.

I don't care about who is going to help you.

I care about the when because if you don't have time for your Middle Goal, the greatest why in the world doesn't matter. "When?" is the first question I asked Melissa C. from Los Angeles, California, one of the research participants for this book. During the study, she shared her desire to tap into more of her potential but also the challenges she faced:

> I am a wife and homeschool mom. I have a contract to maintain the website for our homeschool academy. I teach a class for our co-op days. I have a part-time direct sales business mostly for the discount. I have the desire to write and teach for ministry. I have started learning to play music again. I would love to learn to quilt. I would like my house decluttered and redecorated before our sons grow up and move out. I also need to strengthen my heart. How do I balance the wants and needs?

I went through her question and noted that there are twelve different roles, responsibilities, and goals in there. Maybe you have more, maybe you have less, but your life is busy too.

When we first confront this reality that we have too much to do and not enough time, we march off in search of a magical solution. Perhaps there's a system we just haven't tried yet, a book we haven't read yet, an app we haven't downloaded yet.

Except there's not. I've tried dozens, maybe hundreds in the last twenty-five years. I've spent so much time trying to manage my time, which feels a bit ironic now that I see it written out in black and white—kind of like buying a dozen books on how to be a minimalist.

There's not a solution to your time crunch, but there is something even better. There's a truth that will set you free: *the reason you're busy is that your imagination is bigger than your calendar.*

Your to-do list will always be bigger than the amount of time you have to accomplish it because your imagination is bigger than your calendar. Calendars are flat, small boxes of time. Your imagination is just the op-

Your imagination is bigger than your calendar.

posite. It's infinite. It's bottomless. It's ever changing, ever growing, ever shifting. And then you take your imagination and combine it with the imaginations of the people in your life: your spouse, your kids, your coworkers, your friends, your boss. Everyone you interact with brings their own messy, wonderful imagination into your life with expectations and tasks of their own. The calendar doesn't stand a chance against that!

The next time you feel guilty at the end of the day for not getting everything done, write down that soundtrack on a Post-it note by your computer: *My imagination is bigger than my calendar.* That will definitely make you feel better, but if you want to do better, you need to answer that question "When?"

When faced with Melissa C.'s daunting list, I asked her one question that I would ask you too: "How much time do you have to apply to your goal right now?"

The most common answer to that question is, "I don't know."

Time only moves in one direction. We all know our time is leaving us, but most of us don't know where it's going. You could try doing a time audit. That's definitely a popular reply when asking, "How much time do I have?" You could keep track of thirty-minute chunks for a week or two, each day writing down things like, "My commute was thirty minutes long," "It took me thirty minutes to get the kids ready for school," "I had two hours of meetings," and so on, but that's a fairly overwhelming task.

Though I've experimented with that approach in the past and even did a whole podcast episode about it, for our purposes today, it can be a little discouraging. It's kind of complicated, and it often triggers perfectionism: "I spent thirty-seven seconds getting dressed—better write that down." A time audit is also based off the foolish hope that every week will be exactly the same. But every week is different. The hope that you can map out an hour-by-hour approach to each week isn't realistic. Life is more fluid and dynamic than that.

The big problem with a time audit is that it won't give you a quick win that makes you want to continue, which is what I'm always looking for with any goal. I want a microburst of joy right out of the gate, a bit of instant progress that inspires me to keep going. If you feel like you haven't been living up to your potential, which is going to motivate you more right now—a challenging task or a quick win?

I think we both know the answer. So how do you get that? You steal the first fifteen minutes.

Johnny Depp Doesn't Care about Your Goals

Did you know there are about 30 minutes from the time you sit down on a plane to the time you actually take off? I didn't until I tracked a dozen flights and got an average. The fastest was 22 minutes. The slowest was 1:08.

I flew 500 times in the last decade and never even noticed that half hour chunk of time. That's 250 hours. It takes me around 500 hours to write a book. I didn't notice half a book's worth of time right in front of me. How did I find it? When I started focusing on my potential, I started paying attention and decided to steal my time back.

You can't make more time, but you can steal it.

I can't add another hour to my day. There's no eighth day in my week or thirteenth month in my year. But I can pay attention and steal it back for however I want to use it.

If you walk by me on a plane, expect me to be reading. One of my Guaranteed Goals is to read fifty-two books this year. Unless I steal back those thirty-minute blocks here and there, there's no way I'll have time for that. So while the person next to me on the flight is scrolling through their phone, I'm going to be reading.

There's plenty of time available; usually you just have to steal it back.

During the Johnny Depp defamation trial, I tweeted a quick thought:

@JonAcuff
If you're too busy to work on things you care about but have also spent hours following the Johnny Depp/Amber Heard trial like it was a sad sporting event where everyone loses, I have some good news. You're not too busy. Write your book. Run your miles. Build your business.[2]

You can switch out "Johnny Depp" for "Will Smith Slap" and it still works. That could just be a big fill-in-the-blank with anything the Kardashians have done lately, a fantasy football team, or any other minor distraction.

What's the big deal, right? What's fifteen minutes here or thirty minutes there? The big deal is that it adds up over time. If I fly a hundred times this year, I'll have stolen back fifty hours. That's more than a full workweek applied to something I care about. That's a lot of potential.

So go steal your first fifteen minutes.

Don't look for ten hours. Don't look for that ten thousand hours it will take you to get to expertise.

Find the first fifteen minutes.

Can you carve out fifteen minutes this week to apply to your Middle Goal? There are 10,080 minutes in a week. Can you reclaim fifteen of them?

The answer, of course, is "Yes!" No one reading this would possibly say, "Jon, I want to tap into more of my potential. I'm committed to excellence. I want to change! I just can't find fifteen minutes in a pool of 10,080 minutes. I'm that busy."

I'm not worried about you saying that. That won't be the response to this idea. The response will be, "Fifteen minutes isn't enough time." That's what high performers always say because they want to sprint on new projects.

I agree—on the surface maybe finding the first fifteen minutes doesn't feel like it's enough. But that's because you're forgetting three things:

1. Fifteen is a lot more than zero.

If you worked on your goal zero minutes last week, fifteen minutes this week is infinite. That's the comparison you need to be making, by the way. Don't compare fifteen minutes to ten hours or ten weeks. Compare fifteen minutes to zero minutes. When you do that, you realize, "OK, that's more than none. I'll give you that."

2. **You can change the world with fifteen minutes.**
You can accomplish a lot more in fifteen minutes than you think. Abraham Lincoln's Gettysburg Address was only two minutes long. That speech changed the shape of our entire country in about 120 seconds. It only takes the space shuttle eight and a half minutes to leave the atmosphere. You can put our entire planet in the rearview mirror in less than nine minutes. It only took me about thirty seconds to propose to my wife. It took a lot longer to convince her to say yes, but getting down on one knee, the ring, all of it was pretty fast. There's a lot of life you can fit inside fifteen minutes.

3. **Momentum always starts with the first fifteen minutes.**
The old adage that says "The hardest part of any journey is the first step" is not completely accurate. The middle is the hardest part. The middle of any goal sucks. But the first step isn't easy, especially if any of your fears about your goal have calcified over the years. The blank page for a writer, the LLC paperwork for an entrepreneur, the first yoga class for someone trying to get in shape—all of those can be a bit intimidating. But if you can get to minute sixteen, you're golden. It's unbelievable how fast fear falls away when you're in motion. We think we need a massive runway of time, but usually all it takes to start is the first fifteen minutes.

Perhaps I've convinced you that a mere fifteen minutes holds value, but maybe you've still got that nagging question we all face—where will I find spare time?

The answer is in between.

The Minutes We're All Missing

Susan Robertson recently finished her degree online. That's a fantastic accomplishment! Do you know where she worked on it? I'll let her tell you because she's the one who did all the work: "I utilized the car pickup lane for school!" Not all at once, mind you. That would be the world's longest car pickup lane. Bit by bit, ride by ride, Susan knocked out her degree.

Jason Daily built his entire company while waiting on flights in Atlanta. That airport is bursting with frustration or potential. You can rage against the injustice of a delayed flight to Kansas City, or you can steal an hour back for a new company.

Valerie Richter's life is also full of waiting, but she focuses her time on a health game. "I like to work out while waiting," she says. "When I throw something in the microwave or oven, I do wall push-ups or squats or jog in place while waiting."

E. Beck calls that "stolen exercises." She told me, "My favorite is brushing my teeth on one foot to work on balance."

Allison Oran uses her waiting time for a fun game. "I get a good twenty minutes of reading for pleasure done while I dry my hair (I know that's weird)," she said. I have to politely disagree with her because that's not weird. That's wonderful.

Anne Larghe found her extra time where we can all find it: waiting for Zoom meetings to start. "I am always ten to fifteen minutes early, logged on waiting. So fifteen minutes times the number of Zoom calls a week adds up." What does she do? She focuses on her career game. She reprioritizes her task list, writes thank-you notes, fixes conflicts on her calendar, and sometimes even plans meals for the week too.

Jennifer Houg found the in-between time so helpful that she made it part of her daily routine. Here's what she told me: "I get up 20 minutes earlier, take a full lunch break, and do 20 minutes before bedtime. This gives me 100 minutes per day to get it done." Working on her goals between her other commitments has proven to be critical for Jennifer. It's not always easy, of course. She says, "I HAVE to choose it every time because I'm never going to 'feel like it.'" But she's learned something valuable: "Success is in the seconds." Working on her personal goals in between other commitments proved invaluable.

Each of those people has the same calendar you and I have, but they learned something that took me decades to figure out.

Minutes matter.

Even if a Middle Goal grew into a Guaranteed Goal and took years to complete, like earning a degree, they knew those years were made of minutes, and there are a lot of those hidden in every day. Not only do minutes matter, but *minute* actions matter too. When E. Beck found two minutes brushing her teeth, she had a two-minute action she could plug into that moment. When Jason Daily found forty-seven minutes at the airport, he had a forty-seven minutes–sized action for that moment.

That's how Susan Robertson finished her degree online while in the car rider pickup line. She had enough actions that, regardless of where she was, regardless of how little time she had, she could make some progress. She made use of the time, she says, "Even if it was simply listening to audio from a video or the textbook being read out loud." That's why having a flexible Middle Goal is so important.

One of the reasons I've been able to write nine books is that I have that Swiss Army knife of actions. A lot of writers only have a few actions, such as "Write for two hours" or "Do deep research on a topic." When fifteen minutes of time shows up unexpectedly, they don't have an action that fits that space. I do, and you should, too, because it gives you the entire day to play with, not just specific, perfect moments. You also don't waste any time trying to decide what to do. If the person getting their hair cut before me is extra chatty and my appointment is late, no problem. I just found ten extra minutes to read a book on Kindle.

Stealing back minutes from activities that don't deserve them and applying them to intentional actions feels amazing. It will also change much more than just how you think about distractions like social media.

When you start to value your time, you'll realize that stress and worry don't deserve it either. When stress says, "Hey, let's spend an hour focusing on something dumb you said last week," you'll think, "No thanks. I could really do something amazing with that hour." When you're in the pursuit of your potential, stress won't seem like the kind of action that's worthy of your time.

You don't stop worrying. You just start working on your goal and one day realize you have less time for things like stress, fear, and doubt. You care too much about your limited resource of time to give it away casually to something that isn't serving you.

Not only do MINUTES matter, but *minute* actions matter too.

That's one of the core principles of living in your potential. You don't become more disciplined in avoiding things that are wasting your time; you become more devoted to the things that matter and end up enjoying more discipline than you've ever known.

It's Just a Matter of Time

You can accomplish anything if you throw enough time at it. The state of Tennessee taught me that accidentally.

In my state, they require you to drive with your teenager for fifty hours before she takes the license exam. This is a challenging task at first because you're taking your life into your hands for the first twenty-five hours or so. I judged those first hours by how often I almost died and how often I needed to apologize to my kids for yelling, "We're about to die!"

But as I write this, I can see my youngest daughter pulling out of our driveway for swim practice. She drives everywhere by herself now. How did we go from "We're about to die!" to "Will you pick up some milk on your way home from school?"

Time.

You can take a terrified teenager who is convinced they'll never be able to handle a car and turn them into a capable driver in about fifty hours. You know that kid of yours who cut their own hair one day just because you left the scissors on the kitchen counter? The one who short-circuited the entire downstairs to find out what happens when you put a fork in an outlet? The kid who as a preschooler carved "Happy Birthday" onto the side of your car with a screwdriver to surprise you?

That kid is going to drive!

That kid is going to navigate cloverleaf highway overpasses, 18-wheelers, and unexpected thunderstorms in the middle of rush hour. That kid is going to learn how to drive in fifty hours.

What could you do in that amount of time?

What would happen if you threw fifty hours at a new job opportunity? What would happen if you threw fifty hours at a side hustle? What would happen if you threw fifty hours at a less-than-awesome marriage?

Start with the first fifteen minutes. Ease into the adventure for certain, but know this: the better you get at stealing time from the things that don't deserve it, the more time you'll have to throw at the things that do.

Using blocks of time this way is also such a perfect work-around to fear. When fear says, "You can't build a business," don't argue with it. Just change the conversation. Say, "I don't have to build a business. I just have to throw five hours, ten hours, twenty hours, or fifty hours at my game and see what happens."

Can you get in shape? I don't know. But I bet you can set a timer for five minutes and go for a walk. Can you make your entire house sparkle with Martha Stewart cleanliness? I don't know. But I bet you can do wonders with three hours this week. Can you write the authoritative history of the ill-fated *Lusitania*? I don't know. But I bet you can find more inspiration than you ever imagined possible when you spend ten hours exploring the idea.

Time is a resource, but it's also a tool. Whenever I bump into a goal I'm afraid of, I break it into time. When my inbox is out of control, I don't try to reach inbox zero. I decide to work on emails for thirty minutes. When I don't feel like working out in a hotel room in San Antonio, Texas, I set a timer for forty-five minutes and get started. When a book project looms large, I break it down into hours and get started. I wrote this entire book, all six hundred hours of it, in fifteen-, thirty-, and sixty-minute segments.

Steal back your time from activities that don't deserve it. Find the first fifteen minutes and look for the moments in between. When you do, time will stop being a resource that you're always running out of and will turn into a consistent, clear metric that you can use to make consistent, clear progress.

Results Are the Only Thing Louder Than Discomfort

Middle Goals help you avoid the Chaos Zone and steal back your time, and they may even turn into Guaranteed Goals, but I have to warn you—they will feel foreign at first.

Pacing my performance instead of sprinting and stopping felt like writing with my left hand the first few times I tried it. It was uncomfortable. I'm still a rabbit at heart. I didn't want to waste my time with the middle of the goal ladder. I wanted to grab that top rung and crush Guaranteed Goals!

Discipline didn't stop me from doing that; the results of trying a few Middle Goals did. Days turned into weeks, weeks turned into months, and I could see the progress other people and I were making. The approach worked. I turned my career around. I started consistently writing books and running half-marathons. I was no longer that failed college student misusing every bit of potential I had, and all it took was a goal.

But right as things really started to take off, everything almost blew up in my face because I was using the wrong fuel and didn't even know it.

THE FUEL

10

Find Your Favorite Fuel

I wish that we only had to get unstuck one time in our lives. I wish that once we visited the Potential Zone we automatically stayed there forever. I wish the lessons we learned were retained forever the very first time we learned them. But a rich, full life is usually a series of escapes from the Comfort and Chaos Zones, not a singular event.

By 2019, I'd become an author, a goal that started as a third grader at Doyon Elementary School in Ipswich, Massachusetts. I was traveling the world sharing ideas with companies, I had my own business, and I felt a million miles from the Comfort Zone I'd escaped with my blog nearly a decade earlier.

On paper everything was great, but trouble was on the horizon, and my wife saw it sooner than I did. A few days after I signed the best publishing contract of my entire life, a moment that should have been peak Potential Zone, Jenny said something surprising to me: "Jon, you're a jerk during the two years when you write a book, and you're a jerk during the two years when you sell the book." (She didn't actually say "jerk," but I'm trying to keep this book family friendly.)

We talked for an hour in the kitchen that day, and she ended the conversation with a sobering proclamation: "This ain't it. This doesn't work for our marriage. I'd rather you be a happy plumber than a miserable writer." It took me about a week to understand what she meant.

In order for me to buckle down on a big project like writing two books, I had to fire myself up. The only way I knew how to do that was with stress.

Crisis was my fuel. Chaos was my fuel. Fear was my fuel.

I couldn't get inspired unless things were so desperate that I had no other choice. I had to back myself into a corner, cut off all means of escape, and wait until the deadline was breathing down my neck before I'd get motivated.

In Aesop's fable, the rabbit didn't run for the joy of it. He ran out of the panicked realization that he was about to lose. That's how I operated too. The bigger the project, the more fuel I'd need to finish it, and thus the bigger the chaos I had to create to motivate myself. In order to get through a four-year book project, I had to crank up my stress levels to 100.

Have you ever worked with a leader who is great at putting out fires? In times of crisis, they shine. They rise to the challenge, prevent the disaster, and save the day. But what happens when there's not a fire for them to focus on? They feel useless, and leaders don't like that feeling. What do they do in that moment? They create a fire so that they can feel valuable again. Now you don't have a leader in your midst—you have an arsonist.

When I share this idea in speeches at corporations, this is the one that makes people elbow each other or look at a boss sitting nearby. It's an uncomfortable truth, and it's the Chaos Zone at its finest. Instead of yo-yoing back and forth between the Comfort Zone and the Chaos Zone, you just set up shop at the turbulent end of the spectrum. It's like moving to the Vegas strip. It's bright, it's loud, it's stressful, and at first it makes you feel alive.

That's the problem—it's not an issue at first. In fact, putting out a fire in your life can be a healthy form of inspiration.

In the 1980s, Richard Beckhard and Reuben T. Harris developed a popular formula that represented what real change requires. The formula is D×V×F > R. The D is your *dissatisfaction* for how things currently are. The V is your *vision* for the future. The F is the *first steps* you're going to take. And the R is your *resistance* to change.

When your dissatisfaction is deep enough, your vision is big enough, and your first steps are clear enough, you'll overcome the resistance and actually change.

A doctor who warns you of future health issues if you don't make changes to your lifestyle is using dissatisfaction to motivate you.

A boss who fires you is offering you a chance to prove her wrong with how well you do at your next job.

A significant other who breaks up with you is giving you one of the most common reasons people join the gym.

The pain leads to change, which is great. At first.

But it eventually fails as a sustainable fuel for the following reasons:

1. The pain ends.

Hopefully, the crisis has a conclusion. You lose the weight the doctor suggested. You get a new job after being fired. You pay off the credit card. Even a pandemic dissipates. When it does, if pain is the only source of fuel you have, you're left with a bittersweet feeling of "Now what?"

If pain is your reason to change, when you're no longer in pain either you quit or you manufacture a new crisis. A president of a talent agency once told me he was having trouble with an employee who was still living in survival mode. During the pandemic the company had reduced staff, and this employee had to do the job of three people. He crushed it for a season, saving the day in his small department and riding the wave of that crisis to success. A year later, even though the company had restaffed, the employee was still operating at panic speed. He was refusing to admit he no longer had to do the work of three people. Instead of sharing responsibilities with his new coworkers, he was frantically storming through projects and dropping balls left and right. The pain had ended but his use of it hadn't, and he was causing significant issues in an office that was no longer in crisis.

2. You forget the pain.

My first root canal was the worst experience of my life. I hated every moment and swore I'd brush my teeth religiously from that moment on. I was bound and determined to never have another root canal. And yet I did. That pain might have motivated me for a week or two of new behavior, but eventually I forgot about it. The further I got away from the pain, the less effective it was as a source of motivation. The pain of last year's root canal wasn't enough to inspire me to floss today.

3. The pain turns into bitterness.

If your goal is to prove someone wrong, it's nearly impossible to emerge from that experience unscathed. Unprocessed pain often turns to bitterness. You end up waging a war that no one else is fighting. The old boss you're trying to beat probably forgot you exist. The ex-girlfriend is now married with two kids and broke up with you mostly because she was an immature college student who didn't know how to have real relationships yet. The dad you're trying to earn praise from might have passed away ten years ago, but you keep holding on to his approval as your source of motivation. Pain as a fuel eventually hollows you out instead of filling you up.

Despite intellectually knowing all of that, I would've kept using pain and crisis as a fuel. It's hard to let go of a fuel source when you've trusted it for years, especially if you've been successful. But then my wife told me I was miserable to be around, my stress levels started turning into physical health issues, and all the joy of the dream job I'd worked so hard to build felt more like drudgery.

I was stuck—again.

I wanted to tap into more of my potential, but the only way I knew how was with a fuel that eventually would burn me up. Even the space shuttle drops the booster rockets once it leaves Earth's atmosphere. "A solid fuel source helps rockets with the initial thrust, but once ignited, solid propellants burn continuously, limiting the number of applications."[1] In other words, once it's started, you can't dial down the solid fuel source; you can only drop it completely.

At that point, astronauts switch to liquid propellants that "can be started and stopped at will throughout a mission, which makes them the best candidates for space travel."[2] Solid rocket fuel, much like crisis, has only one function—to help you escape the atmosphere you're in. If you really want to go to new levels, you can't rely on it.

I was all rocket boost but had whole universes I wanted to explore. I needed a new fuel.

Potential Zone Fuels

Fifteen years ago, while we were standing on a patio in Alpharetta, Georgia, a friend asked me a surprising question: "Why does your father-in-law still work?"

At the time, my father-in-law was in his early fifties but had accomplished a lot since his first job of digging sprinkler systems right out of high school. Despite never finishing college, he had risen through the ranks of multiple businesses and was the area president of the second largest privately held home building company in the country. He managed hundreds of millions of dollars of projects and had, by many definitions of the word, "arrived." I was still caught off guard by my friend's belief that he should retire at fifty-two though.

"He doesn't have to work. He could just play golf and coast," he continued, musing on an obvious option my father-in-law was apparently missing. "Why does he still work?"

It's a good question that you can ask about anyone who

is successful. Why does Oprah still work? Or Jeff Bezos? Or Warren Buffett? It can't be the money.

Do you think Warren Buffett works so hard because his goal is to get to $200 billion? Do you think he'll quit when he hits that? Nope. Money has long ceased to be the driving force in his life. That's why in 2006 he pledged to give it away. "More than 99 percent of my wealth will go to philanthropy during my lifetime or at death." Strong words for someone worth more than $100 billion, but he gets even stronger when he describes why he's doing it: "Were we to use more than 1% of my claim checks (Berkshire Hathaway stock certificates) on ourselves, neither our happiness nor our well-being would be enhanced. In contrast, that remaining 99% can have a huge effect on the health and welfare of others."[3]

The pursuit of money might have started Buffett's career, but he's long since switched to a more sustainable fuel. At some point in the journey, high performers always make a switch from short-term fuel to long-term fuel if they want to stay in the Potential Zone.

The Potential Zone is special. It doesn't run on regular fuel. It only accepts four types:

1. Impact
2. Craft
3. Community
4. Stories

If those words feel a little bit familiar, they should. They're the best versions of the ideas you found hidden inside your Best Moments List.

Potential Zone Fuels

1. Impact
2. Craft
3. Community
4. Stories

Your best *accomplishments* will *impact* the world.

Your best *experience* comes from pursuing your *craft*.

The best *relationships* always lead to *community*.

The best *objects* tell a *story*.

Those are the four most powerful, most sustainable fuels for succeeding at your Middle Goals. Middle Goals are challenging. If you really want to work on something for thirty to ninety days, you need much more than just the trick that got you out of the Comfort Zone. You need a fuel.

If the majority of your best moments were relationship-based, guess which fuel will inspire you the most? Community.

If experiences filled your list, can you imagine which of the four will motivate you? Craft.

If accomplishments lit you up, so will impact.

If you were a mix of all four, then get ready for a unique mix of all four fuels. Everyone uses them a little differently.

Warren Buffett runs on impact. Elon Musk thrives on craft. Oprah Winfrey believes in community. And you? Well, let's find out together.

I probably won't end up a billionaire. I might not make it to Mars. I'll likely never get to scream, "And you get a car!" But if I'm going to tap into the 50 percent of me that's just waiting to go, I need the right fuel, and so do you.

11

Achieve the Best Kind of Accomplishment

At age 28, Scott Harrison had it all. A successful club promoter in New York City, he drove a BMW, had a grand piano in his Manhattan apartment, dated models from the covers of fashion magazines, and spent his weekends bouncing from Milan to Paris to London. His job was simple: pack beautiful clubs with beautiful people who would pay $1,000 to drink a $40 bottle of champagne. And he was good at it. Budweiser paid him $4,000 a month just to be seen drinking their product out in public. He was an influencer before the internet even really existed. After a childhood spent taking care of an invalid mother, he was living the big city dream, and he had it all—right up until his short-term fuels started to sputter out.[1]

You can accomplish wonderful things with fame, money, and power, but they're better as a consequence for a life well lived instead of as a cause for living your life. In his late twenties, Scott came to a place that most wildly successful people don't reach until much later in life.

"I realized, wow, there would never be enough," he told me when I interviewed him on my podcast. "If I died, there would be no purpose for my life. My tombstone would read, 'Here lies a club promoter who got a million people wasted,' full stop." I don't know if they'll even carve such a depressing statement on a tombstone, but Scott knew he wasn't tapping into his full potential—not by a long shot.

"I was emotionally, morally, and spiritually bankrupt," he said. In that moment, he had more than enough dissatisfaction and pain to overcome his resistance to change. Scott didn't want to sit in that spot anymore. "I wanted to reinvent my life completely and see if I could find purpose, to see if I could be useful."

Can I be useful? Can I make a difference? Can my life matter? Questions like that are often the front door to one of the best fuels we all have access to: impact. But how do you do that as a club promoter? It's a fairly vain set of skills and not the background you'd imagine a world changer possessing.

Scott was stuck, but he did have a degree in photojournalism that he'd barely acquired. "I was a C–/D+ student," he admitted. (Turns out I'm not the only one who squandered college.) With a camera and charisma, Scott talked his way on board a hospital ship headed to Liberia, the poorest country in the world. He didn't have a perfect plan. He didn't have a ten-year vision. He just knew that the Comfort Zone wasn't working so well anymore, and he was in too much pain to stay the same.

In Liberia, the Mercy Ships ocean liner full of medical personnel set up a hospital in a soccer stadium with 1,500 slots for medical care. As Scott stood there capturing this first experience, he was stunned to see that more than 5,000 people showed up. "We sent 3,500 sick people home with no hope because we didn't have enough doctors and we didn't have enough resources. I remember weeping because I later learned that these people had walked for more than a month from neighboring countries just to see a doctor. They were bringing their kids with them from Sierra Leone, Côte d'Ivoire, and Guinea, just hoping that maybe a doctor could save their child, and we didn't have enough doctors."

It was Scott's first real shock in West Africa, but it wasn't his last. "When I went into the rural areas, I saw people drinking dirty water for the first time in my life. You have to contrast this with the idea that I sold VOSS water for $10 [a bottle] in our clubs just weeks before."

As the days rolled on and Scott's humanitarian education continued, a statistic stood out to him that offered a possible solution to all the hardship. "I learned that 50 percent of the disease in the country was caused by unsafe water, a lack of sanitation and hygiene. It was a eureka moment."

He ran back to the ship and talked to the chief medical officer, who had been working in that area for twenty-five years. "I told him, 'People are drinking water that is killing them,' and he said to me, 'Why don't you go work on that problem? I'm going to help thousands of people every year using my hands through surgery, but you could be the greatest doctor in the world if you just got 700 million people clean water.'"

You can interpret a moment like this one of two ways. It's either an impractical dream with insurmountable odds or an inexhaustible fuel for change. Scott chose the latter.

When you get a glimpse of the impact you can make, the size of the problem becomes your ally because it means your drive to solve it will never quit.

Scott returned to New York City with fresh wind in his sails. He didn't have a detailed plan for his nonprofit, so he started his mission with what he had.

> **The size of the problem is your ally because your drive to solve it will never quit.**

"The only idea I had was to throw a party in a nightclub for my birthday. I figured I could get a club and an open bar donated for my friends." You usually don't have to become an entirely different person to change the world. You often just have to use the gifts you already have but in slightly different ways.

Scott sent out an email that said, "It's my 31st birthday. Come to the meatpacking district in New York, and make a $20 donation to get in the club." That casual party was the first day of Charity Water, and they ended up raising $15,000 in cash that night.

Fifteen years later, Scott and Charity Water have raised $700 million to bring clean water to almost 15 million people in 29 countries.

That's impact, a fuel that will not run out, and you have the exact same access to it that Scott does.

Finding Your Africa

When you hear amazing stories like Scott's, it's difficult not to immediately think, "I could never do that." Me neither. That's actually the same response Scott would've had if you had tried to tell him the middle of the story when he was in the beginning of it. If on that day when he was crying in a soccer stadium as he watched parents carrying their sick children home you had said, "Don't worry, Scott, you're going to raise $700 million and change the world," he wouldn't have believed you.

He would've said the same thing you might be thinking right now: "I could never do that." He wasn't ready for that reality. All he was ready to do was throw a party in a nightclub and try to see if this thing could be a thing. That's how impact always starts. It's small and it comes in many different forms.

You don't have to raise $700 million to change the world. Sometimes all you have to do is send a text message. If you want to change the world, encourage one person today. I tried that Middle Goal one month. Every day I'd text something encouraging to one person. Out of the blue, I'd send a text like, "Was just thinking today about how amazingly creative you are. Whenever I talk with anyone about art or innovation, you're the example I use!"

To this day, I've never had someone say, "I wish you hadn't sent that text. This was the worst moment to tell me that."

They usually respond with just the opposite. "You had no idea how much I needed that today. That made my day!"

A text that costs you sixty seconds and thirty words can make someone's day. Impact usually has a 100× ROI. You get so much more back than you put in.

Whether you're fighting for clean water for the masses, or texting one friend, or something between those two extreme ends of the impact spectrum, if you can see the difference your goal is making, you'll work on it longer.

Getting in shape impacts your family. I run in part because the endorphins I get make me a lot nicer to be around for my wife and kids.

Paying off your credit card debt impacts your community. When your high school marching band does a fundraiser, you'll have money to donate. An awkward sophomore you'll probably never meet will discover a love of music that carries them through the difficult years of high school because you helped the administration buy a tuba.

If you can see the difference your goal is making, you'll work on it longer.

Starting a podcast will impact someone in a country you've never been to because you were brave enough to share the story about your parents' divorce on an episode.

Every time you dare to step into your potential, you cause a bigger impact than you can possibly imagine. That's one of the reasons impact is such a good fuel for staying inside the Potential Zone. It's always available and never runs out. To tap into it, start by asking this question: How does this accomplishment impact the world?

If you work in health care, for instance, it's easy to get overwhelmed by the stress of the job. Government regulations are always changing, the hours are long, and the consequences are tremendous. Doctors, nurses, and health-care administrators don't get to say the two sentences most of us get to say when we're stressed out: (1) "It's not life or death" and (2) "It's not brain surgery." In many cases, working in health care *is* life or death.

One afternoon, I asked a roomful of overwhelmed hospital staff an impact question: "Who are you doing this difficult job for?"

It was quiet for a few seconds until one woman raised her hand. "I do my job for the 'donor walk.'"

I wasn't familiar with that phrase, so I asked her to explain. She said, "When someone is going to donate an organ, we call it a 'donor walk.' The entire staff lines the halls—the nurses, the doctors, the administrative team—and we all clap as they're wheeled into surgery. That's why I do my job."

On days when it's difficult, at times when she doesn't feel like working on Middle Goals or even Easy Goals, that woman remembers that her work is impacting that moment. She's part of the donor walk, and the donor walk saves lives.

When I ask teachers who they are doing their difficult job for, they always say something that's similar and at the same time completely unique: "I do my job for the me I used to be. When I was in middle school, my parents went through a divorce that devastated me. My grades plummeted, my attitude cratered, my life fell apart in every possible way, and there wasn't a single teacher who noticed. I'm a teacher for the me I used to be because I'm going to make sure I show up for that kid who's like me."

That's impact. If you ever feel like you're running on fumes, spend a few minutes and reconnect with it. Somebody's life is better for the work you're doing. If you can't find a single example of that, it might be time to get on a boat headed for Africa—or at least send one friend an encouraging text.

When the Impact Tank Is Completely Empty

A friend called me one afternoon with a career dilemma. He'd recently had an ordinary experience that left him with some extraordinary questions. You can't schedule eureka moments; they tend to show up according to their own schedule. This one happened while he was painting a ballet studio in exchange for some free lessons for his daughter.

During the long, hot hours brightening up the space, he found himself thinking, "I like painting a lot more than I like my job." He had a great position at a financial company in Texas, but he couldn't see the impact of his work as clearly as the impact of painting that little studio.

For years to come, the studio would feel fresher and more welcoming because of his work that afternoon. That was impact. As he sat with this thought—as you should always do when you get an unexpected glimpse of the Potential Zone—he remembered how much he loved power washing driveways. He'd spent one summer soaked and happy with his kids as they served neighbors. Then he remembered that during COVID, he and his family made thousands of dollars together by cleaning out dryer vents in their community.

Painting was the first best moment he caught, but others tumbled out as he worked on his list. Each one of them involved manual labor and tangible impact. He called me with the question we've been asking this entire book: "How do I get more of that?"

His tank was empty but not in a bad way. This wasn't a midlife crisis. He just noticed something was missing. You might too when it comes to this fuel discussion. If you do, follow my friend's lead and go back to your Best Moments List or start a new one. Look at your accomplishments (impact), experiences (craft), relationships (community), and objects (stories).

You never have to be limited by your past. On the contrary, you can be set free by your past—especially when it's helping you put more best moments in your present and your future.

If the tank ever feels empty, don't worry. You know the best person to refill it.

You.

12

Get Crafty without Any Glitter

Brendan Leonard will never win the New York City Marathon. It's not for lack of trying. Despite titling his book *I Hate Running and You Can Too*, he's a dedicated ultrarunner. One year, for instance, he ran a marathon distance every week. I'm not saying he ran a total of 26.2 miles every week. I'm saying he did a 26.2-mile run every week, or the equivalent of 52 marathons in a year.

He's not going to win the New York City Marathon, though, and you won't either. He's comfortable with that because that's not the point of this endeavor. "You won't ever find yourself telling your grandkids, 'I got 33,789th place that year, but if a couple of things had gone a little differently for me, I could have gotten 32,372nd place," he says. And when you tell your coworkers you ran the New York City Marathon, none of them are going to ask, "Did you win?"[1]

Brendan runs for the joy of running. He runs for the challenge. He runs to compete against the version of himself that didn't think he could do it. He runs to get better at the craft of the activity, which is a fuel that's every bit as motivating as impact.

George Mallory, the famed mountaineer, summed up craft best when a *New York Times* reporter asked why he wanted to climb Mount Everest: "Because it's there."

Whether you win or lose, whether you ever get to see the impact, whether anyone even knows you did the thing you're doing, you're going to keep doing it because the joy of getting better propels you. I asked thousands of people what they do just for the joy of doing it, and the answers revealed how many different ways you can interpret the word "craft."

Keith Eastman, a marketing manager at a trailer manufacturing company in Boise, Idaho, will never open a restaurant, but that's not why he cooks. "I really enjoy bringing in a new tool and getting better at using it to achieve maximum finished quality." He likes the gadgets, he likes the recipes, and he likes the challenge of new ingredients. He loves cooking because he loves the craft.

Alex Ferrero, a sales adviser in Nashville, will never have a chicken empire. But if you ask him why he loves chickens, he's quick with an answer. "It helps feed our family, teaches our kids care and responsibility, and is relaxing." You can buy eggs anywhere, but an egg from your own chicken is a completely different thing. It's a craft.

Chris Sherry, a stay-at-home mom from Port Orchard, Washington, isn't going to sell her knitting, but she could. "Everyone always tells me I should sell my work, but I just enjoy figuring out a new pattern or stitch and then giving that piece away to someone I love!" It's her craft, not her career.

Joelle Sprott Yates, a former elementary schoolteacher in Tyler, Texas, will never play the piano at Carnegie Hall. But that's not why she plays. She said she loves "learning a difficult piece just for the satisfaction of it." That's the heart of what a good craft involves—satisfaction in the effort, not just the results.

Julie Chenoweth Terstriep, a farmer in western Illinois, will certainly never make a job out of her craft. "I love cleaning the military tombstones in cemeteries. I try to find out more information about the serviceperson and their family history. It's a way for me to say to them 'thank you for your service.'" The family of the deceased might never know. The fallen veteran doesn't know. But Julie knows, and that's enough.

One of the best parts of having a craft you do just for the joy of doing it is that it doesn't have a natural conclusion. That's the very definition of a long-term fuel. You never "arrive" because there are always new levels to achieve.

You never "arrive" with a craft because there are always new levels to achieve.

Ashley Varland, an assistant vice president in insurance operations, explained it perfectly: "I'm working on my MBA now, which I plan to finish, but I'll never stop reaching for a resource and testing my knowledge. I don't do it for the letters behind my name. I genuinely enjoy learning!"

You might accomplish something tangible by dedicating yourself to your craft. Alex is teaching his kids responsibility with the chickens. Chris might sell her knitting someday. Ashley is earning her MBA. The difference is that the results are a consequence of your action, not the cause of it. It's a benefit, but it's not the reason you're doing it.

In a corporate setting, this is often called "engagement." Employees will stay at companies for less money, longer commutes, and smaller titles if they believe in the work. If they've got a craft they love doing and, even better, can tie that to a real impact their job is making in the world, they'll stay on a team for decades. On the flip side, if they can't figure out a craft at their job, they'll quickly become bored, disconnected, and in some cases bitter about the work. Another company offering $1 more than they're currently making can woo them away.

The mistake we often make with craft is confusing it with a hobby or an activity that is naturally enjoyable. It can be both of those things, but the real power of the fuel is that you can turn anything you do into a craft.

In his book *Finding Flow*, professor Mihaly Csikszentmihalyi tells the story of Rico, an assembly line worker at an audiovisual equipment factory. His only job was to inspect movie cameras for quality four hundred times a day. Csikszentmihalyi writes, "Although he had to do the same sort of boring task as everyone else, he had trained himself to do it with the economy and the elegance of a virtuoso."[2]

The company allowed Rico forty-three seconds to check each piece of equipment, but guess what he did? He turned it into a game. He spent years honing the process with different tools and actions until he was able to inspect each camera in twenty-eight seconds. He didn't get an extrinsic reward. The rest of the line moved at the same speed it always did, and his coworkers probably thought he was weird, but Rico didn't care. "It's better than anything else," he said, "a whole lot better than watching TV."[3]

Rico turned his job into a craft. He wasn't spending years on an assembly line. He was spending years in his Potential Zone. "And because he sensed that he was getting close to his limit in the present job, he was taking evening courses for a diploma that would open up new options for him in electronic engineering."[4] Why did Rico approach his job that way? The same reason Mallory climbed Everest. Because it was there.

You might never work in a factory like Rico. But if you'd like to get good at something you *want* to do or enjoy something you *have* to do, the path is the same—turn it into a craft.

To make a task a craft, ask yourself questions like this:

Can I do it better?

Can I do it faster?

Can I make it more enjoyable?

Can I do it in fewer steps?

Can I create something new if I add or remove a part?

Can I measure and track my performance?

The more questions you ask, the more answers you'll find as you turn a short-term action into a long-term craft.

When Your Craft Gets Taken Away

I shared the idea of craft as a fuel with a small team of leaders in Dallas, Texas, when I was writing this book. You can instantly tell if an idea is working based on how people react to it. If they politely nod along during the presentation—or worse, check their phones—it's not there yet. If they wait for you while you

To get good at something
YOU *WANT* TO DO
or enjoy something
YOU *HAVE* TO DO,
TURN IT INTO A CRAFT.

JON ACUFF

#AllItTakesIsAGoal

pack up your laptop and then follow you to your car to ask additional questions, you might be onto something. Which is exactly what one executive did that afternoon.

"This makes so much sense to me," he said. "I've been frustrated at work because my craft got taken away." I hadn't considered that you could lose a craft and asked him to elaborate on that idea.

"I got promoted," he said, "which is great, but with the new role, I'm no longer able to do the things I love the most at my job." Now I understood what he meant because I had seen that at every company I'd ever worked for.

In Atlanta, I worked with a graphic designer who was great at creating beautiful websites that perfectly balanced form and function. She loved pixels like Picasso loved paint. She enjoyed getting her hands dirty each day, throwing on a pair of massive headphones and wiling away hours with Photoshop and Illustrator. That was her craft.

She was so good at design that she got promoted to creative director. That meant she no longer got to design but was instead managing designers. Her reward for being good at her craft was that she no longer got to do it. This frustrated her because upper management essentially said, "You know the thing you love? You no longer get to do it and you have to watch other people do it."

Tony Romo didn't join the announcing booth in the middle of his career. That would've been torture for him just like it was for my friend. Her design career wasn't over; it was taken away from her.

She was also the worst micromanager. She couldn't help redesigning all her subordinates' work because she missed doing it herself in the first place. Her colleagues dreaded showing her projects because they knew she was going to change everything.

You don't have to work in a big organization to experience this problem. I wrestle with it every day in my own small company.

I've run my own business for the last ten years. Writing is my craft. Creating ideas and then sharing them in speeches, books, podcasts, and social media is my favorite thing to do. It's also the thing I try to ruin on a fairly regular basis. I don't mean to, but when I talk to other business owners and they ask me how many staff I have, I get embarrassed. I want to say one hundred. I want to say that we have a cool building in a cool part of Nashville. I want to say that we have a huge office Christmas party where I give everyone a TV and they get to take their picture with reindeer I've hired from wherever it is that you hire reindeer.

I think I'm supposed to scale and staff up, but every time I try, I find myself losing access to the craft. My writing time disappears in the onslaught of meetings, people, and projects. Three months in, I look up and ask myself, "Why am I so frustrated right now?" Then I realize I've stopped doing the thing I love the most when it comes to my career game.

I have a friend whose craft is scaling businesses. When I toured his office in Las Vegas, he had four different companies churning out products and services. He loves hiring and managing people. Conversely, he hates writing books. If he spent a few hours every day writing, he'd be miserable. I'm just the opposite.

If craft is the fuel that moves you and you feel disconnected from some part of your life, make sure you haven't stopped doing the thing that matters most to you. Those last two words are the most important on this whole page: TO YOU.

Make sure your craft fits who you are and make sure your calendar reflects that you're giving it time. If you're not, don't worry—you can fix that quickly. Just reread chapter 9 and steal back those first fifteen minutes.

13

Find Your People, Find Your Potential

I don't want to run most Saturday mornings at 6:50 a.m.

After a full week, hitting the road for five miles on the first day I can sleep in doesn't sound fun.

Spring is too rainy for running.

Summer is too hot for running.

Fall is too dark for running.

Winter is too cold for running.

I'm an excuse machine on Saturday mornings, but I still get up. It's not grit, discipline, or willpower that motivates me. Those three amigos let me down constantly. What gets me out the door is my running group.

I know that at 6:50 a.m., Rob Sentell is going to be sitting in my driveway. I know that at 7:00 a.m. we're going to pick up Kevin Queen together. I know that at 7:05 a.m. all three of us are going to meet Justin Johnson in the YMCA parking lot to head down the river trail. I know that at 8:35 a.m. I'm going to come bursting through the front door of my house like the Kool-Aid Man, so glad I did a run I hadn't wanted to do initially.

Community will call you back to the Potential Zone when comfort and chaos try to distract you, and I have more of it in my life right now than I've ever had before.

Every other Wednesday I meet with William, a buddy who is helping me with a big goal. On Wednesday nights, Jenny and I go out to dinner with three other couples who have kids the same

Community will call you back to the Potential Zone when comfort and chaos try to distract you.

age as ours. Every other Friday I meet with a small group of dads from my neighborhood who are in the same stage of life I am. On most Saturday mornings I run with the Ginkgo Eagles. (That's the name of our running group. We have T-shirts. It's a thing.) Twice a month Jenny and I meet with a small group of eight couples in our neighborhood who we've known for a decade. Once a week I go for a walk with one of my good friends Nate or Ben. Throughout the week I also have meetings with my team, clients, and prospects, and I see a performance coach every six weeks.

It wasn't always this way. The first year I started my business I gave isolation the old college try. I holed up in my home office, counted the thirty-second conversations with my dry cleaner as meaningful interaction, and responded to text messages at the speed of never. I wish there were an emoji for "I saw your text but didn't know how to perfectly respond to it so I waited until I knew exactly what to say but it's been three weeks so now I just feel microbursts of shame every time I see your name in the elephant graveyard of messages on my phone."

I tested isolation as a life strategy for a solid year, and I'm here to tell you something you might have figured out already: it doesn't work. You probably already knew that, but for perhaps the last time in this book, I will remind you, I am a late bloomer—even when it comes to the value of community.

One afternoon, a thought hit me while driving through Chattanooga, Tennessee. That's a good city to do some thinking in because the highway was designed by someone who apparently hates humans and loves gridlock. The main passage through Chattanooga is carved into a treacherous mountain pass and includes a nearly ninety-degree turn. I've never driven through Chattanooga quickly in my entire life.

While I sat there, I looked around at other people in other cars and realized it only takes one person to drive a car down the highway. You don't need a team for that. A single man or woman can helm a Honda Civic on the interstate at 65 miles per hour.

But if you want to drive a Formula 1 car at 223 miles per hour in races in Dubai, if you want to take corners on the oceanside streets of Monaco at 186 miles per hour in a $12.2 million vehicle, it takes up to 1,200 people. They're not all in the cockpit, but if you ever watch a Formula 1 race, you'll be amazed at how many people it takes to get that car around the track in peak condition.

By the time I made it home to Nashville, I had made a decision. I wanted to be a Formula 1 car, not a Honda Civic. I wanted to go farther and faster than I'd ever gone before. When you've accomplished a few Middle Goals, you always feel that way. You've had a taste of what's possible, and you don't want to go back to the Comfort Zone or Chaos Zone. If I was going to stay in the Potential Zone, I was going to need a lot of people.

Because categories help me simplify complicated ideas, I decided to categorize the relationships that inspire me in five ways:

1. Family
2. Clients
3. Peers
4. Coaches
5. Inner Circle

Here's how I define them:

Family = Immediate and extended

This is the easiest to define. Your family consists of your immediate and extended family. Immediate family is your spouse or significant other and your children. Extended family is your mom, dad, siblings, cousins, grandparents, and so on. I have two kids, one wife, two parents, two brothers, and one sister. I also have in-laws, cousins, uncles, aunts, nieces, and nephews.

Clients = Anyone your work serves

You don't need to own a business to have clients. If you volunteer at a food bank, you have clients. If you sell insurance, you have clients. If a neighbor asks for advice about a conflict with another neighbor, you have clients. If you're a third grade teacher, you have twenty-five short clients each weekday. If you have a podcast, you have clients. If you write a book, you have clients. (Thanks for being one of mine!) If your efforts help anyone, you've got a client.

Peers = People who overlap at least one game

A peer is someone you share at least one of the five games with (career, finances, relationships, health, and fun). Maybe you're in the same career or at the same stage of relationship life. Maybe you both have young kids or you share a fun hobby like rooting for the same college team. You might share multiple games, but there's always at least one connection with a peer.

The older you get, the less time you'll want to spend with people you don't share anything with. That's why, in a friendship between two married couples, it's a miracle when all four spouses truly like each other. There's always that awkward scenario where one spouse has a best friend married to someone their partner only tolerates to make them happy. The really amazing moment is when the spouses all get along and the kids get along too. It's always disappointing when you discover that a couple you love is raising jerks and your kids become jerks every time they hang out.

You could use the term "friends" for this category instead, but I prefer peers.

Coaches = A wise person who is ten-plus years ahead of you in either age or experience

Simply put, a coach is someone who is further along than you. Maybe they've been married twenty years and you've only been married ten years. Maybe they've worked in your industry for thirty years and you're just starting out. Maybe they're younger than you but have more experience in a craft. Chris Zimmerman, who helped me with my YouTube channel, is twelve years younger than me but has spent ten years building YouTube channels, so he's a coach for me.

The word *wise* is important here because a coach needs to have achieved something you want to emulate in your own life. You need to be able to look at them and think, "Oh, I want that for my own life too." This is not hard to figure out, because fruit is loud. Either the fruit of their decisions will generate tangible peace, patience, and excellence, or it will generate chaos, hurry, and incompetence.

Inner Circle = People who know you at your worst and still think you're the best

This is the smallest circle of all. There are only a handful of individuals in this category for most people, myself included. This is someone who knows your whole story and still thinks you're pretty swell. This is the first person you call when something amazing or something terrible happens. In rapper terms—because I'd like to offset that I just used the word *swell*—this is your "ride or die."

Those are the five categories of community. When I was describing them, did anyone instantly come to mind? Did someone's name pop up in your head? Good, because you've already got a head start on identifying your community.

If community is a fuel that motivates you, it's important that you be intentional about it. Can you come up with the names of three to five people who are in each of those categories?

Family will be easy. I'd write down Jenny, L.E., McRae, my brothers, my sister, my parents, and my in-laws. Creating a list of clients will be easy too. Just make a list of the last five people you helped.

Peers might be a little more challenging, but I think you'll be surprised how easy it gets as you go. I once told one of my coaches that I didn't have a lot of peers, and he started rattling off names of people I'd mentioned to him over the last year. I went home after that conversation, spent about fifteen minutes with my notebook, and wrote down eighteen different people who came to mind. One thing that helped was looking through my contacts list on my phone.

The coaches category will require you to think about the future a little bit. Don't limit yourself to coaches you currently spend time with. Also write down a few you'd like to spend more time with. Right now I meet with Carey Nieuwhof once a month via a thirty-minute phone call. He's ten years older than me in marriage, age, and podcasting. He's someone I can learn a lot from on a lot of different levels. David Thomas, who I mentioned in my book *Soundtracks*, is a coach I'd like to spend more time with. We've only had one coffee together, but if you've read my book, you'll remember it really impacted me. I don't know how to make that happen because David has a really busy schedule, but I'd add his name to my list.

The last category, the inner circle, is in some ways the easiest to spot and the hardest to build. It's the easiest to spot because you definitely know who you'd call if something amazing or terrible happened. It's the hardest to build because it takes a lot of effort.

There will definitely be overlap, with some people fitting in multiple categories, so don't get stuck on that. For example, my friend Stephen Brewster is in my inner circle, he's a peer, and he's a coach. I could put him in any of those categories, but for the point of this exercise, I'd put him in the deepest, the inner circle.

If labeling your relationships feels a bit extreme, I agree, but the world is currently built to keep you isolated, so an extreme response is called for. This isolation started in the 1960s when televisions began offering more than three channels. Paul Graham points out what a big shift this represented for community: "It's difficult to imagine now, but every night tens of millions of families would sit down together in front of their TV set watching the same show, at the same time, as their next door neighbors. What happens now with the Super Bowl used to happen every night. We were literally in sync."[1]

We've sacrificed community at the altar of convenience.

The feeling of separation has only increased as we've sacrificed community at the altar of convenience. Services like Door-Dash and Uber Eats are amazing, but they effectively eliminate your ability to be known by someone at your local restaurant. That was the hook of the theme song for the show *Cheers*: "Sometimes you want to go where everybody knows your name."

On the day I wrote this, I started the morning at my local coffee shop. The barista grabbed a cup and started my order before I even reached the register. I asked her how old her son was because I hadn't seen him at the shop for a while. It wasn't a long, meaningful interaction, but we both walked away from that with the sense that another person on this planet had seen us. If I had mobile-ordered, I would've received my coffee a little faster, but I would've been order number 3455 in the system, not "Jon, the guy who always gets the same thing every Friday morning."

Netflix killed Blockbuster, but it also eliminated movie recommendations from an employee who was often a film buff.

The pandemic killed your commute, but it also eliminated unplanned lunches with coworkers and microinteractions that make teams strong.

Grocery store delivery killed the hassle of walking the aisles, but it also eliminated the sixty-second interaction with Peter, the eighty-year-old retiree who decided to be a bag boy late in life.

Peloton killed the inconvenience of attending a spin class with a fixed start time and limited space, but it also eliminated grabbing a smoothie with Jill, the young mom who's trying to raise toddlers right now too.

Zoom killed in-person meetings, but it also killed the ten-minute catch-up conversations that happen before and after real meetings, which build real working relationships. No one hangs out after a Zoom meeting is over. I'm focused squarely on trying to convince my brain to not wave goodbye at the end of the Zoom like I'm Forrest Gump on a shrimp boat.

It's starting to sound like I make my own butter, but I promise I'm pro technology. According to my Screen Time app, I use my iPhone on average 6 hours and 58 minutes every day. I enjoy the convenience of technology, but I have to admit it comes with a cost.

You didn't have to work as hard to build community twenty years ago because life naturally provided it. You ran into neighbors at the grocery store. You interacted with a dozen coworkers in the breakroom. You knew the manager of your local restaurant because you came in at least a few times a year for an hour-long meal with your family. You saw the same people at the six a.m. aerobics class, and if you missed a few times, they might even reach out to you.

But accidental community is over. The future is intentional. We just haven't realized it yet.

In 2000, renowned leadership expert Peter Drucker made a prediction that grows truer every day:

> In a few hundred years, when the history of our time will be written from a long-term perspective, it is likely that the most important event historians will see is not technology, not the Internet, not e-commerce. It is an unprecedented change in the human condition. For the first time—literally—substantial and rapidly growing numbers of people have choices. For the first time, they will have to manage themselves. And society is totally unprepared for it.[2]

Technology offers us the choice to either isolate or congregate. Never before have we had to manage that choice like we do today.

Accidental community is over. The future is INTENTIONAL.

If you feel isolated, make a different choice.

If you feel disconnected, make a different choice.

If you feel that you've reached the edge of your abilities and you need a fresh set of eyes on what you're working on, make a different choice.

Invest in community, especially if your Best Moments List taught you that your relationships are important to you.

14

Own More Stories
and Fewer Objects

When you reviewed your Best Moments List, was it full of objects? I have a guess: nope.

I bet that when you categorized your list, objects was one of the smallest of the four categories. How do I know? Because that's what happens to everybody.

Denis Cockerham had only two objects on his entire list.

Joyce Ernst said, "Objects was my smallest category." There were only 33 objects on her list of 183 items.

Brooke T. had 26 objects on a massive list of 350 items, which means only 7 percent of her best moments were focused on objects.

There were only fifteen objects on my list. I was surprised by how few people really cared about objects, because advertising tells us just the opposite. Modern marketing is predicated on convincing you that you don't own the right objects yet. Advertisers tell us, "As soon as you have this new object, you'll feel complete, special, and different. Acquiring that object as fast as you can should be your goal. It's the only fuel you should use to drive your life."

But when we reflect back on the best moments of our lives, we rarely think about the objects. The objects we spend our lives acquiring don't give us the lives we're desiring. I promise that will be the last rhyme in the entire book, but it's true. I'm not about to argue for minimalism. I love my car, my LEGO sets, my laptop, my books, and plenty of other objects. I'm pro-object. But if you're going to use an object as a fuel, it's important to draw the line between the right object and the wrong object.

The difference is simple.

The right object is a story.

The wrong object is just an object.

There's always a story in a right object. When I looked at my Best Moments List, there wasn't a single object on it "just because." Each one was meaningful and significant.

Look at the objects you added and I bet you'll find the same thing to be true. If you and I had coffee and I asked, "Why did you put that object on your Best Moments List?" do you know what you'd say? You'd say something like, "My dad gave me this watch. His father had one, and when I turned eighteen he felt like I should have one too." Or you'd say,

> **There's always a story in a right object.**

"I bought this purse because I promised myself that when I hit my sales number at work I would get a reward." Or maybe you'd say, "I had one of these as a kid and always wanted to get one again when I was an adult. I know it's silly to be excited about a box of baseball cards when you're in your fifties, but I am."

The details might be different, but you'd be able to tell me the story behind that object. And it wouldn't be just any story. There are actually five main stories we tell when we talk about objects. Each one is connected to the way the object makes us feel.

Story 1: This object makes me feel young.

Story 2: This object makes me feel successful.

Story 3: This object makes me feel inspired.

Story 4: This object makes me feel cool.

Story 5: This object makes me feel connected.

You're probably already smiling because reviewing your list of objects made you feel one of those ways. But let's break down the stories so we can really use them as a fuel.

Story 1: This object makes me feel young.

There were three objects on my list that made me feel young:

1. The Porsche 911 GT3 RS LEGO set
2. The Benchmade knife
3. The 64-pack of Crayola crayons

All of those make me feel like a little kid again. Any object that harkens back to the childhood you had or—this is important—the childhood you *wish* you had, fits into this category.

Why did fanny packs boomerang back into demand? Why did *Stranger Things* become so popular? Why did *Top Gun: Maverick* become Tom Cruise's first billion-dollar movie?

Because they all captured nostalgia. Each item won over a new generation, but it also reminded an older generation of childhood. Every time my daughter hears a 1980s song and says, "That's from *Stranger Things*," I think, "No, that's from my childhood."

As you think about a fuel that will help you with your Middle Goals, ask this question: "Are there any objects on my list that make me feel young?"

Story 2: This object makes me feel successful.

Do you know why I bought myself a pair of skis? Because they made me feel successful. When I was young, we didn't have a lot of money. We were by no means poor, and I don't want to overdramatize my childhood, but my dad was a pastor and my mom is a dental hygienist, so there wasn't a ton of cash for something as frivolous as fancy ski trips.

I remember being at an airport once when I was in the third grade and seeing a family headed West to a ski resort. They were covered in neon ski gear and looked like they were on the edge of an adventure. I told myself, "Someday I will be successful enough to own a pair of skis." The teenage cashier who eventually sold them to me at Sun-n-Ski thought it was just another retail transaction, but for me it felt like crossing a finish line thirty years in the making.

In the same way that some relationships can fall into more than one category, most objects tell more than one story. For example, the Porsche 911 GT3 RS LEGO set makes me feel young, but it also makes me feel successful. It cost $400. I couldn't have purchased that when I was a kid. I never even saw that amount of money all together, never mind have it available for a toy car. But as an adult, having the ability to spend that much money on something like a LEGO set makes me feel successful. That's why I bought a skateboard too. You feel like you're high-fiving the eight-year-old version of yourself when you're able to buy the things you always wanted.

This is one of the reasons it takes courage to share objects you enjoy, because someone is going to say, "I would never spend $400 on a LEGO set. What a waste." But brush that off. It's your Best Moments List, not theirs. I would never spend $1,000 on a purse or $125,000 on a car, but if those are objects that move your world, go for it.

Story 3: This object makes me feel inspired.

There are some objects you own because every time you look at them you feel inspired, creative, and hopeful. You might have a small painting on a wall in your home that makes you feel that way. If you're a cyclist, maybe your bike does that for you. It's sleek and aggressive, without a wasted line on it. Every time you see it, you want to go faster and faster. Just walking past it in the garage on your way inside from work gives you a little dopamine hit.

The object might inspire you by reminding you how big and beautiful the world is. That's why people collect seashells. That's why I have a bowl of acorns. They don't make me feel young or successful; they make me feel inspired. As I wrote in chapter 3, an acorn is the perfect picture of potential.

Walking into a bookstore, an art supply store, or REI can make you feel inspired. Those are collections of objects that speak to possibility. Here's a book that could change your life. Here's a canvas you could fill in. Here's a kayak that will float you down the river.

Some objects are fuel because they're a reward for finishing a goal. My friends Lindsay and Michael Moreno buy Super Bowl tickets every time their business hits a big financial goal. Some objects are fuel because they inspire you during the goal. That standing desk you splurged on motivates you to keep working on your thesis. The inspiration an object provides can come before, during, or after the project.

Story 4: This object makes me feel cool.

Cool is the younger cousin of successful. They're related, but they're not exactly the same.

Cool is personally defined. For example, my wife Jenny has a pair of pants she loves. She wore them just the other day and always gets compliments on them. Do you know why she loves them? Because she got them at Walmart.

She loves surprising people who ask where she bought them. For her, looking like a $1,000 but spending $10 is a win. That's something she'd put on her Best Moments List. No one would say, "Look at Jenny, she's so successful, she's able to afford pants at Walmart."

But cool is personal. Pulling out a notebook on a plane to write down an idea makes me feel cool. It makes me feel like a real writer who is capturing some brilliant inspiration in the sky. The person next to me probably thinks that's dorky. Wouldn't a laptop or an iPad be more practical? Maybe, but you get to define what's cool to you.

Story 5: This object makes me feel connected.

These are objects you own that make you feel connected to another person. They can be mementos, but they don't have to be. For example, I have an old Bible on my bookshelf that was my grandfather's. My dad gave it to me when my grandfather passed away. When I see that Bible, I feel connected to both of them. When I read the notes my grandfather wrote in the margins, I feel connected. There are objects you have that become reminders of people you love.

But the connection can also mean you're connected to a whole community of people. I used to work with a guy who was an intense Disney fan. He and his family would go to Disney World twenty times a year. I lived in Atlanta at the time, so that wasn't a particularly easy trip. One day, he told me about a message board he belonged to called the Green Mickeys. It was an uber fan club that had an object they all identified themselves with.

They would go to Home Depot and get a green Disney paint sample card that was in the shape of the mouse ears. At home, they'd cut out that green Disney logo and laminate it. The next time they'd go to the park they'd put that laminated card on their hotel door, their baby stroller, or even on the back of their hat so they could quickly identify themselves as part of that community. That paint chip—an object—made them feel connected. A Harley does the same thing. A Big Green Egg does the same thing. There are dozens of examples of objects like that.

Now, if our goal were to declutter our house, we'd use those five stories to edit our closets. It would be like an extreme version of Marie Kondo. Instead of asking, "Does this spark joy?" we'd ask, "Does this object make me feel young, successful, inspired, cool, or connected?" If you go 0 for 5, maybe you don't need to own that object.

The real power of understanding the five stories, though, is that it increases your self-awareness. When you know the objects you really care about, you can intentionally add more of them to your life going forward. That's the beauty of the Best Moments List. It reveals our past, informs our present, and prepares our future. Don't try to use objects as a fuel if they don't motivate you.

Maybe when you read the list of five stories you thought, "I don't care about feeling cool, successful, or young. I just want to feel connected." Fantastic! Shape your purchases around that story. Wave to every other Jeep owner you see because that object makes you part of a community.

Maybe you're just the opposite and love feeling young at heart. That's a big part of your value system. That's why you collect comic books and Star Wars memorabilia. That's great too. My friend Shawn spent more than $1,000 on an official Darth Vader costume. When he wears it in parades, little kids lose their minds. That makes him feel like a kid again too. Did saving up for that help motivate him with some of his career goals? You bet.

Maybe feeling inspired is your number one story. I overspend on books and notebooks for exactly that reason. To me a book feels like a passport to a new life. That's where a lot of my time and money go.

When you add the right objects to your life that tell the stories that inspire you, it's a lot easier to work on your Middle

Goals. And the right object can even be tied to your other categories.

I bet most of the objects on your list were related to experiences, accomplishments, and relationships.

Skis make me feel successful. That's an accomplishment.

Bukola Okoro's fridge magnets aren't just holding up paper. "My fridge tells a full story of my travels," she says. That's an experience.

For Kerri Simonin, a fancy pair of shoes was really about a relationship. She says, "My shoes from the Barney's sale in NYC wasn't about the shoes (although they are awesome). It was about my first trip with one of my girlfriends to NYC."

Objects can be a great source of fuel when they tell a story and when they're connected to something deeper. If you know the type of objects you care about, the best ad for the latest gadget won't sway you an inch. You'll be so busy living in the Potential Zone and acquiring the stories that matter to you that you won't even make eye contact with that shiny distraction.

The Four Fuels

I'm still tempted to use chaos as a fuel sometimes. To say I've kicked the habit completely would be an exaggeration. When we met with our financial adviser recently, he showed us that we were on track for our retirement plans.

I pointed at the video monitor on the wall in his office and said, "I don't know who that chart you're showing us is about, but I'm going to pretend it's not me so that I can keep hustling when we leave today." That part of me who used stress and disaster as a source of motivation refuses to go down without a fight. But the longer I lean into the healthier fuels of impact, craft, community, and stories, the easier it gets to trust them.

Do you know which of the four fuels motivates you the most? I do.

I'm still tempted to use chaos as a fuel sometimes.

I could tell you that answer right now if you showed me your Best Moments List.

Impact is an accomplishment. The world is different because of something you did. That's the very best type of accomplishment.

Craft is an experience. Regardless of the outcome, the time you experienced doing it makes the moment worth it. Maranda Engstrom researches building codes and comes up with her own designs for schools, apartments, and offices. "I have no training and will never see these built, but it's so fun!" She lives for the craft of it.

Community is a relationship. That one is so painfully obvious that it needs no explanation.

The right objects always tell a story.

If you want to see what fuel will drive you today and tomorrow to stay in the Potential Zone, just refer back to your tally of accomplishments, experiences, relationships, and objects. I had 61 accomplishments, 59 experiences, 35 relationships and 15 objects on my list. Clearly, the two fuels that drive me are impact and craft.

The best part of my day is the three to four hours I spend alone writing new ideas. I have dozens of notebooks with tens of thousands of ideas in them. I love seeing how many ideas I can come up with in a month the same way Rico loved seeing how fast he could inspect movie cameras on the assembly line.

When I travel for work, I hole up in my hotel room and write as many ideas (craft) as I can to help as many people as I can in books, speeches, and courses (impact). My friend Carlos Whittaker is just the opposite. When he visits a city, he organizes a meetup with his "InstaFamilia," gathering as many strangers as he can from Instagram for a rambling conversation in a coffee shop.

We're each using different fuels in different ways, but the result is the same: more time spent in the Potential Zone. Everyone will approach these four fuels in their own unique fashion, and no one ever just uses one fuel. You'll benefit from all four at some point in your life.

When you start to use them more deliberately and spend more time in your Potential Zone, a funny thing happens: The future is no longer intimidating. The Vision Wall disappears. You've learned from your past with the Best Moments List. You've crushed a few Easy Goals to break out of the Comfort Zone. You've avoided the Chaos Zone with some Middle Goals. And now you're ready to answer the question we raised back in chapter 1:

How do I live in the Potential Zone full-time?

Anyone can visit for a few hours, a long weekend, even an entire month or two.

But how do you make your home there?

How do you open every gift you have?

How do you do all of that and so much more?

With Guaranteed Goals.

THE PROMISE

15

Guarantee Your Success

I am going to sell one million books during my career. Less than 1 percent of authors accomplish that, but I guarantee it's going to happen.

In the next twelve months, I'm going to be physically stronger than I've been in the last ten years. That gets harder to accomplish every day, since I'm almost fifty and find myself tempted to use my iPhone's flashlight to read restaurant menus, but I guarantee it's going to happen.

By the end of the year, I will have read thirteen times the number of books the average American reads in the same time period. That's not easy to do when you're writing your own book, raising kids, and running a business, but I guarantee it's going to happen.

Before the fourth quarter closes, I will have found an extra $50,000 in my business by spending fifteen minutes a week looking at a one-page document. That's an awful lot to expect from a single piece of paper, but I guarantee it's going to happen.

On December 31, my wife and kids will tell you that despite focusing on all those other goals, I was a better husband and father than I was last year. This is starting to feel like a nearly impossible task list, but I guarantee it's going to happen.

I'm not cocky about what I'm capable of. My natural insecurities probably make yours look microscopic in comparison. I also don't believe you can just "speak your truth into reality." Words without work are useless. Those aren't predictions; those are promises. If anything, I probably underestimated. It's hard to fully grasp what you can accomplish when you spend more of your life inside the Potential Zone.

If you're a rabbit like me and you've been waiting to pick up the pace, congratulations—these next three chapters are going to be your favorite in the entire book.

The Painfully Obvious Magic of Guaranteed Goals

Easy Goals get us out of the Comfort Zone.

Middle Goals help us avoid the Chaos Zone.

Guaranteed Goals keep us in the Potential Zone.

The only problem is that no one thinks Guaranteed Goals really exist. That phrase feels like an oxymoron. How can you guarantee something that exists in the future when the future hasn't happened yet?

Our discomfort with the words *guaranteed* and *goal* is not a new issue. We've been dealing with it for more than 230 years.

"There are no guarantees in life but death and taxes" is one of those Ben Franklin quotes that got remixed a bit. The original quote is from a letter he sent to French scientist Jean-Baptiste Leroy in 1789, where Franklin wrote that "in this

WORDS
without
WORK
are useless.

---

world nothing can be said to be certain, except death and taxes."[1]

That statement is true-ish. There are very few guarantees in life, and social media is full of people selling you promises they certainly can't deliver on. "Make seven figures in passive income in 20 minutes of work a week!" "Lose 92 pounds forever just by cutting one food out of your life that doctors say is terrible for your feet!" "Build a crypto empire with NFTs like this 22-year-old billionaire who sold a doodle of a skunk for $19 million! (He's not even that good at drawing skunks!)"

You should be very skeptical of anyone offering guarantees. I know I am. But we can all agree that there are more guarantees in life than just death and taxes.

For instance, it's a guarantee that the best way to find a guy with a leaf blower is to start recording a podcast. Nothing makes your neighbor start doing yard work like the need for a quiet Zoom meeting. A guy who rented a jackhammer from Home Depot "just because" will materialize out of thin air the minute you finally get a baby to sleep.

Those are guarantees. The world is full of them, and despite popular belief, there are even Guaranteed Goals. What are they? Goals where the efforts ensure the results.

With Guaranteed Goals, the efforts ensure the results.

If you put in the work, it's impossible for you to lose.

If you lean into the process, the product always follows.

If you give it time, the reward always happens.

That's the magic of Guaranteed Goals, and it's always painfully obvious.

How do I know, not just hope, that in the next twelve months I'm going to be physically stronger than I've been in the last ten years? Because if I do 150 CrossFit workouts this year, it will be impossible for me not to get into better shape. I haven't worked out with weights in ten years. Guess what will happen if I work out with them 150 times this year?

I didn't start my fitness journey with that goal. It was too big. My stuck self would have mutinied if I said, "You know how we haven't consistently worked out with weights in a decade? Well, now we're going to do it roughly every other day for a year!"

I wanted to approach the goal that way on day 1. Of course I did! I'm the king of the Chaos Zone, after all, but even old rabbits can learn new tricks.

I also didn't think about 150 workouts when I was working on my Middle Goals. I wasn't ready then either. I didn't have a foundation yet and would have sprinted right into the Chaos Zone and said something like, "Now that I've done three workouts, I'm ready for 300!" I would've maintained that pace for three weeks, burned out, and then given it all up.

Instead, for my Middle Goal, I tried twelve workouts in a month. I accomplished that and then tried fifteen. I accomplished that and then tried twenty. Around the third month, I started to suspect that maybe I could do 150 in a year, but I took my time. I knew my trainer Caleb was right that I'd be tempted to overdo it and injure myself, so I kept turning Easy Goals into Middle Goals until eventually I was ready for the best goals of all—Guaranteed Goals.

How did I know I was ready? I had proof. The wins you get with your Easy Goals become evidence that you're ready for Middle Goals. The wins you get with your Middle Goals become evidence that you're ready for Guaranteed Goals. You don't have to guess if it's time to level up some part of your life. The results make it obvious.

Not every Easy Goal turns into a Guaranteed Goal, but every Guaranteed Goal should start with an Easy Goal.

For example, Katie Coric, a clinical social worker from western New York, had an Easy Goal to transfer money from a 401(k) at a previous employer to her current employer's 401(k). She had been putting it off, she says, because it "seemed daunting, but ended up not taking too long." It took about an hour of active work, which is easy. Katie won that small finances game but didn't need to turn that into a Middle Goal or a Guaranteed Goal. She didn't start managing her money differently for the next ninety days or become an accountant. She had been stuck in the Comfort Zone and used an Easy Goal to get out.

> **Not every Easy Goal turns into a Guaranteed Goal, but every Guaranteed Goal should start with an Easy Goal.**

Remember, it's a goal ladder. Only about 10 to 20 percent of the goals progress up a rung. I'll try hundreds of Easy Goals. They only take a few minutes or days, are generally free, and have obvious steps. Responding to one email I've been avoiding, putting the laundry away, cleaning out my car, changing a light bulb that's been out for six months, buying vitamins, updating my passwords once a year—life is full of Easy Goals.

About ten of those will be so meaningful and fun that I'm willing to invest in them a little more. I'll turn those into Middle Goals. Now that I've got the vitamins, I'll commit to taking them every day for a month. An idea I wrote about for a week will be worthy of a few more weeks of writing. A few conversations with a business coach will turn into a ninety-day commitment.

A few of those ten Middle Goals will become Guaranteed Goals that I'm willing to really work on.

Which ones? Well, they must have these five factors:

1. **Guaranteed Goals have extended time frames, usually ninety days to a year.**

   Quick wins are awesome. They help you leave the Comfort Zone. But potential is about sustained performance over time. We're not trying to visit the Potential Zone; we're living there. So a goal with a long time frame actually works in our favor. One of my Guaranteed Goals right now is to spend eight hundred hours this year crafting new ideas. I want to write a new book every year, and I know it takes me roughly five hundred to six hundred hours to do that. If I focus on the eight hundred hours of crafting ideas, at the end of the year I'm guaranteed to have a new book done. I can't rush that goal. Some weeks I may only get eight hours in, but if I'm faithful to keep chipping away at it, the results are guaranteed. (You can see all the hours I track on my Instagram account, @JonAcuff.)

   Here are a few other examples of long-range goals:

   Launching a new product at your company.
   When I worked at Bose, it would take us about twelve to eighteen months to bring a new speaker system to market. That could easily qualify as a

Guaranteed Goal. We couldn't guarantee how many would sell. We couldn't guarantee supply chain issues outside of our building. But if we spent twelve to eighteen months taking a new product through our highly refined system, we were guaranteed that the result would be a new speaker. We had decades of Easy Goals and Middle Goals as proof we were capable of that. Businesses are full of goals with naturally long time frames.

A vice president of marketing at a software company told me that when he was hired, the CEO refused to let him create any marketing for the first six months. All he wanted him to do was get to know the team. The VP, a rabbit who was ready to run, said it was challenging for the first few months, but eventually he recognized the wisdom of that plan. If he spent six months learning about the team, the company, and the culture, it would be impossible not to be a better VP at the end of the process. That was a Guaranteed Goal.

Training for a marathon.
It takes between sixteen and twenty weeks to get ready for a marathon. It's often easy to see long time frames in fitness goals like that. It takes time to lose weight. It takes time to gain muscle. It takes time to get comfortable on a bike or a rowing machine. Accomplishing any significant

goal always takes a significant amount of time. It also takes flexibility, which Guaranteed Goals provide.

For instance, what if you get injured when you're training for your marathon? Do you give up? No. You pause, recover, and then find a different race to run. That's the difference between a standard goal and a Guaranteed Goal. A standard goal says, "I will accomplish this goal by this date." You really don't know that though. A knee injury might knock you out for three months. A Guaranteed Goal says, "I will train for a marathon for sixteen to twenty weeks." If an injury happens, you haven't missed the goal. You've just moved the weeks forward until you can do them. You might need to sign up for three marathons just to do one, but I guarantee when you finally do it, you'll feel like a superstar who is living in the Potential Zone.

Learning how to plant a vegetable garden.
"Harvesting ten pounds of asparagus" isn't a good Guaranteed Goal. I know too many farmers who laugh at people who think they control the soil, the weather, and the neighborhood deer. But "*learning* how to plant a vegetable garden" is a great Guaranteed Goal because if you put in the effort, it will be impossible at the end of that 120-day asparagus cycle not to know more about that slow-growing plant.

Saving up for a family trip to Hawaii.

Hawaii is open. They let people like you and me go there all the time. I guarantee if you save up enough for a trip, they will allow you to visit. It took my friend ten years to do that, saving up faithfully for a big trip with his family of six. COVID canceled it, so he spent another year waiting to get there. When you've worked on a goal for eleven years, do you think anything is going to stop you? If every airline decided not to fly to Hawaii anymore, he'd probably swim at this point.

The beauty of a long time frame is that if you're living in your Potential Zone, the length of time doesn't make you restless, it makes you relentless.

It will take me at least twenty-two years to hit my goal of selling one million books. My friend Greg McKeown, however, had a rocket-ride book. He had a single book, *Essentialism*, sell more than a million copies. That's amazing, and I am now finally happy for him. I was mostly just jealous until I met him and realized he is completely unhateable.

I've never had that experience. I've written eight books and sold a total of 800,000 copies. To hit my total goal, I'll need to sell 200,000 more. That's just a few more books. If I write a book a year, I'll hit that goal in my midfifties. Even if it takes me three years longer than I anticipate, I'll accomplish that goal before I'm sixty.

I'm not discouraged by that, because I didn't make that Guaranteed Goal before I wrote my first book. I waited until I had written eight books and had already worked through hundreds of Easy Goals and dozens of Middle Goals. Then, when I had evidence that I was on the right track, I was ready to say, "I'll spend the next ten years to hit my million sold goal."

Now the long time frame actually inspires me because it feels amazing to be inside the Potential Zone. The results are going to come—maybe faster than I expect, maybe slower—but in the meantime I'm using way more of my gifts than I used to. I'm adding best moments to my list left and right. I hate waiting. Who likes it? But waiting in the Potential Zone doesn't feel like waiting. It feels like the best party you've ever been to.

That's how I feel after a good writing session or CrossFit workout. I'm exhausted but elated. And then, at the end of the six months or one year or even twenty-two years, I get another big present: the accomplishment. That's a guaranteed good way to go through life.

2. **Guaranteed Goals are 100 percent in your control.**
If you put in real effort, the results are math, not a miracle. Do you know who has 100 percent responsibility for how I treat my wife and kids? Me. It doesn't matter if I have a bad day, get stressed out at work, or am tired from too much travel—I have a choice: to be kind or not to be kind.

There are plenty of goals that are outside my control and therefore don't make for great Guaranteed Goals. For instance, I don't control hitting the *New York Times* Bestseller list. That goal is 100 percent out of my control. I control putting together a book launch team though. I control writing a marketing plan. I control finding fifty podcasts to be on before the book comes out. But the *New York Times* Bestseller list is based off a private algorithm that they keep very close to the vest.

One year I tried to come up with a Guaranteed Goal to walk twenty-six times with a close friend. (I can't read menus, I like going on walks, I pick up acorns . . . I am a thousand years old.) It passed the first test—it was a long time frame. If we walked together every other week, it would take us a year to accomplish it. The only problem was I didn't control his schedule. He started traveling more for work, which almost immediately made the goal impossible to achieve. A better way to make that a Guaranteed Goal would have been to change it from "walk with Matt 26 times" to "ask Matt to walk 26 times." I 100 percent control my ability to free up time on my schedule and be the one who reaches out.

Brenna, a vintage clothing store owner from Ithaca, New York, doesn't control the exact number of items her online store sells in a year. She's not a wizard. But that's not her Guaranteed Goal. Instead, she says, "I'm currently trying to consistently list at least five to ten items per day with a minimum goal of two thousand listings per year." The result she wants is a thriving on-line store. She knows that if she accomplishes her goal of listing a minimum of two thousand vintage items such as clothing and children's books, it will be impossible for her not to achieve that goal. Brenna is focusing on what she controls, and at the end of the year she's bound to see results.

Real estate isn't the same thing as vintage clothing, but it can be a Guaranteed Goal too. It takes about seventeen different people visiting a model home in a new neighborhood to get three appointments with a sales agent. It takes three appointments to find one buyer. You can pull the thread even further and say, "One thousand people need to see the ad to get seventeen of them to come to the open house." I might not technically control the number of people who buy a house, but if I know how many people it takes to start the ball rolling at the top of the funnel, I can control how many ads I run. That's a lot closer to a Guaranteed Goal than just, "I want to be a great real estate agent!"

3. **Guaranteed Goals are easy to measure.**

I have five Guaranteed Goals this year, one for each of the big games:

Career: Spend 800 hours crafting ideas.

Finances: Spend 15 minutes each week reviewing my company's profit and loss sheet, and average three positive actions per review.

Relationships: Be kind to my wife and kids 365 times.

Health: Do CrossFit 150 times.

Fun: Read 52 books.

Do you notice what these all have in common? There's a number associated with each one. If you can't easily track your Guaranteed Goal, you'll get bored with it and you'll either start some other goal, which is Chaos Zone behavior, or you'll give up, which lands you right back in the Comfort Zone.

My initial relationships goal was to be a better husband and father, but that's as fuzzy as goals come. I can't measure that. Do you know what I can do though? I can be kind to my wife and kids 365 times this year. Over the course of twelve months, I can do 365 small, medium, and large acts of kindness for the people who matter most to me.

I came up with that goal when I noticed that my wife was doing a lot of "prepare Jon in advance" monologues. Before we went to a dinner party she'd say, "I don't want you to be grumpy, so let me set some clear expectations. Three of your friends will be there, we're only going to stay two hours, and the people hosting the party own a cool dog you can definitely pet. Can you mentally get your head around that?" It was like she was pre-soothing an irritated gorilla.

Then I also noticed that when I was kind to people and engaged in conversations, they seemed genuinely surprised. "It was nice to have Jon so present tonight!" one friend told my wife and me at the end of a dinner party. I didn't want to get bonus credit for the days I wasn't a jerk. I just didn't want to be a grouchy husband or dad anymore. If I did 365 kind things for my wife and kids in a year, guess what would happen at the end of the year? I'd be a better husband and father. That I could measure.

If your Guaranteed Goal doesn't have a number associated with it, keep digging until you find one. For our previous example of "learning how to plant a vegetable garden," I would refine that to:

1. Spend one hour each week in the garden.
2. Learn how to grow three types of pepper plants.
3. Write down 52 things I learned this year about my garden.
4. Find three coaches who can give me gardening advice.
5. Read five books about gardening in my type of climate.

If you did any of those things and actually measured them, it would be impossible for you not to become a better gardener at the end of the year. That's a guarantee.

4. **Guaranteed Goals force you to be more deliberate.** If I'm going to spend 800 hours this year crafting new ideas, my schedule has to change. This is not confusing; this is just math. There are 8,720 hours in each year. If I sleep an average of seven hours per night, I have 6,205 hours to play with. To hit my goal, I'll need to be crafting ideas one out of every 7.7 waking hours. That is

daunting and inspiring. Once you've woken up to what's possible with some Easy and Middle Goals, you're going to want bigger challenges, and that's a big one!

If your Guaranteed Goal doesn't force you to be more deliberate, you don't have a Guaranteed Goal yet. I had to get very intentional in order to find those sixty-five hours of time each month for crafting ideas. I had to find at least thirteen hours a month for Cross-Fit. I had to trade Instagram scrolling time for reading time in order to hit my book goal. I had to schedule a fifteen-minute PNL session each week in order to hit my financial goal. Here's a simple rule of thumb when it comes to time:

Easy Goals: Require 1 percent of your week or about two hours.

Middle Goals: Require 3 percent of your week or about five hours.

Guaranteed Goals: Require 5 percent of your week or about eight hours.

If that seems like a lot, flip the way you're looking at it. You're not saying, "I have to spend eight hours a week on my goal." You're saying, "I get to spend eight hours a week doing something I love!"

Not every Guaranteed Goal takes that much time. My ideas goal is eight hundred hours over a year, but my finances goal is only thirteen hours total. They're vastly different sizes, but each of them requires me to be more deliberate about my schedule.

In chapter 17, I'll show you how to measure your time in the Potential Zone, but for now just know that a Guaranteed Goal comes through your schedule like an icebreaker in Antarctica. It always causes disruption at first, but in the end it creates a path that makes it easier for every other goal to follow.

5. Guaranteed Goals sound impossible when you tell people about them.

Have you ever been discouraged by someone's reaction to your goal? We all have. When Clarissa Sliva told her friend she was going to start getting up earlier and planning her day, her friend responded, "Yeah, but are you actually going to do it?" That reaction really discouraged Clarissa. She told me, "Those words messed with me both when I failed and even when I succeeded (because doing something just to prove them wrong is a horrible motivation)."

Now, we could psychoanalyze why Clarissa's friend said that. Maybe anyone who criticizes you for exploring your potential is secretly terrified that they are failing to live up to their own. We could come up with elaborate boundaries that Clarissa needs to keep that friend at arm's length. Or we could just flip that discouragement into a sign that she's actually found a good Guaranteed Goal.

A Guaranteed Goal is going to stretch you, which means it's also going to stretch some people's belief that you can accomplish it. When you tell a friend an Easy Goal, they should say, "Is that all?" When you tell a friend a Middle Goal, they should say, "Good for you!" When you tell a friend a Guaranteed Goal, they should say, "Are you sure?"

A good Guaranteed Goal should sound too weird, too ambitious, or too impossible to other people. "I'm going to spend eight hundred hours crafting ideas this year" probably sounds way too big to most people.

"I'm going to spend seven years getting my BA while raising two kids and working full-time" sounds way too long to most people. (But Lin Bedell Ristaino did it!)

"I'm going to take up Olympic weight lifting at age forty and set a state record after four years of training" sounds unlikely to most people. (But Kathryn Little MacKorell did it!)

"I'm going to change careers from truck driving to piano tuning" sounds like way too big of a job jump to most people. (But Ronald Moore did it!)

"I'm going to be kind to my family 365 times this year" sounds way too weird to most people, but I did it.

If someone doubts your Guaranteed Goal, that's not failure. That's confirmation.

There's tremendous freedom when your mission isn't to convince everyone that you can accomplish a goal but instead to get people to doubt you. It's exhausting to get buy-in from people; it's fun to get buy-out. Imagine if Clarissa knew that before she talked with her friend. Instead of that discouragement messing with her, she'd walk away from that conversation thinking, "I must be on the right track."

Rabbits, Rejoice! It's Time to Sprint!

If you want to go faster on your Guaranteed Goal, all you have to do is add a series of deadlines.

Nobody slows down when they can see the finish line in a race. Sales teams marshal every last bit of hustle that's still left in the tank at the conclusion of the quarter. Even college students find extra gears of performance at the end of the semester.

Regardless of your personality, temperament, or background, no one is immune to the magnetic pull of a good deadline. Make sure your Guaranteed Goal has as many as you need.

The first time I tried to spend eight hundred hours crafting ideas in a year, I only had one deadline—December 31. That wasn't enough. It's really easy to get discouraged and bored during a goal that stretches over 365 days with only a single deadline. It's like holding your breath for an entire year.

In June, I realized that on July 1 I would be halfway done with the year. I wanted to make sure I was well over the 400-hour mark so that I was guaranteed to hit the 800-hour total. I also wanted to pad things a little bit, knowing I'd take time off at Christmas. July 1 became a new deadline that fired me up. If a halfway deadline worked, would a three-quarter deadline of October 1 work too? If a three-quarter deadline worked, would a monthly deadline work too? Every time a deadline added motivation, I added another deadline. If you find an approach that works, use it as many times as you possibly can.

I want you to have a massive Guaranteed Goal. I want you to reach for the stars. Don't hold back for a second when it comes to the size or scope of your dream. But if you want to go faster, remember this principle:

Make your Guaranteed Goal as big as possible but the distance between your deadlines as small as possible.

But What About . . . ?

There were dozens of examples of Guaranteed Goals in this chapter, but 99 percent of them were "want-to" goals. They were goals that you'd do out of desire, not obligation. No one was making Kathryn Little MacKorell get into Olympic weight lifting. She wanted to do that. No one is making me read fifty-two books a year. I want to do that. No one will make you grow a vegetable garden. You'll want to do that.

But life isn't all want, is it? You might be sitting in a cubicle right now with a long list of "need-to" goals. Do you want to figure out how to merge two company cultures now that your company has acquired a smaller firm? Maybe not, but you need to. You might not want to get along with a difficult coworker, but you need to. You might not want to learn how to manage your budget better, but you need to.

It's crystal clear that climbing the goal ladder can help us achieve our want-to goals. But what about our need-to goals? Can we even turn those into guarantees? Let's find out.

16

Turn Fears into Goals and Watch Them Fall

I'm afraid of money. On the list of things I fear, it's definitely number one. Here's what my personal list of fears looks like:

1. Money
2. Spiders
3. Spending any amount of time in our crawl space
4. A plane running out of overhead storage before I board
5. Parking under duress

Those last four are fairly easy to deal with. We have an exterminator, so spiders aren't really an issue. I also will empty out my entire 401(k) to pay someone else to go under our house to fix a problem in our crawl space. It's not haunted—that I know of—but scurrying around on my belly in a coffin-height, critter-infested underground labyrinth sounds like a terrible way to spend my day. I fly the same two airlines consistently, so I'm able to board early with my status and always find space for my suitcase. And last but not least, I have that small VW that's easy to park. I've come up with adequate solutions for four of my five fears, but money—that one is a real pickle.

Part of my fear is that someone is going to take advantage of me financially. Who? How? When? Everyone, every time, and always. That's my attitude. You would think I'd been robbed at gunpoint a hundred times or had the bank foreclose on our house annually for how strongly I suspect that something nefarious is going to happen to our money. I'm working on it. My Best Moments List helped with my scarcity mindset, but it's still something I deal with often.

I'm not great at math. I'm a writer. What's arithmetic to you is calculus to me. Figuring out the tip at a restaurant gives me a headache. I'm constantly trying to carry the one, whatever that means. Algebra felt like voodoo in high school. I could barely handle the numbers and then we added letters so that we could ruin the English language at the same time.

I'm also terrified I'm going to make a mistake that ends up with me in prison slowly carving my way out like Andy Dufresne in *The Shawshank Redemption*. I always feel like I'm one financial mistake away from the IRS coming after me. I'm not afraid of snakes, public speaking, or heights, but paperwork makes me sweaty.

This is unfortunate because adulthood comes with a lot of paperwork. If you do it right, being an adult is way more fun than being a kid, but it does require you to manage your own finances.

Ostrich mode is not a great plan when it comes to money, especially if you own a business like I do. A simple rule of entrepreneurship is, "If you don't take care of your money, you don't get to own a business for very long." You can hire all the experts you want—bookkeepers, accountants, financial planners—but at the end of the day, you still need to be involved.

That's true in all five big games you'll play.

You might not want to get in shape, but you need to.

You might not want to go on that business trip, but you need to.

You might not want to repair a broken relationship, but you need to.

You might not want to take a fun vacation, but if you're a workaholic, you need to. (If you're not a workaholic, the idea of *needing* to take a vacation might sound crazy to you, but I assure you that having fun is a hard goal for a lot of people.)

A full life is full of "need-to" moments. They're the unavoidable tasks or projects we'd like to pretend don't exist.

> **A full life is full of "need-to" moments.**

What's the thing you'd rather avoid? I bet it's different from mine. Maybe you do HVAC work and laughed at my inability to mess around in a crawl space. Maybe you're an accountant and money is your playground. Maybe you're a truck driver and parking a rig into tight spaces is something you excel at.

Maybe there's a different game that sends you into an automatic tailspin every time you think about it. Your career has stalled out. You're hoping that you can ignore losing a few pounds and that modern science will eventually fix your health with maybe, like, lasers or holograms. You're an island right now because you don't know how to invest in relationships. Fun is a foreign word because your entire identity is wrapped up in work and you don't see the value in play. Everybody has something they'd rather just not think about but need to.

Now it's time to flip our question from chapter 6 upside down. Instead of looking at the five games of career, finances, relationships, health, and fun and asking, "What game do you want to play?" we're going to do the reverse.

What game are you avoiding?

Up the Ladder We Go

Frogs jump out of boiling water, even if it starts out cold. I don't know why scientists had to explain to us that this popular motivational metaphor was false, but they did. If you put a frog in lukewarm water and slowly increase the temperature, the frog hops out. Doug Melton from the Harvard University biology department put it even more bluntly than that: "If you put a frog in boiling water, it won't jump out. It will die. If you put it in cold water, it will jump before it gets hot—they don't sit still for you."[1]

So instead of regaling you with the thousandth incorrect story about a frog in boiling water, I'm not going to ask you what water in your life is slowly getting hotter. I'm going to keep our streak of simple questions alive and just ask: *What game are you avoiding?*

The list isn't long. Which of the five big games are you refusing to even make eye contact with right now? Which one are you putting off until tomorrow? Which one has your significant other tapped you on the shoulder about once or twice or a million times?

This is perhaps the least confusing exercise in the entire book. A candidate will scream for your attention if you dare to ask that question.

Money wouldn't shut up when I asked it. Like a castaway on an island in the Pacific, it started shouting as soon as I looked through the games. "It's me! It's finances! Can you hear me? Are you seeing me? I spelled out 'HELP!' with coconuts! Would you prefer I light a signal fire? Would it be helpful if I set your whole life on fire to get your attention?"

What game are you avoiding?

I had hoped some other adult would fix the situation. There's always a moment in your life where you temporarily forget you're the adult. "We need a new air conditioner for the house? Who pays for that? Wait . . . I do? There's not some other adult who handles that? It's me? And it doesn't increase the value of the house because people just expect it to have an air conditioner? Fantastic!"

This was one of those moments. I was forty-six years old and beginning to suspect that no one else was going to show up to magically fix all my finances for me. I assumed this was that thing I kept hearing other people talking about called "personal responsibility."

The law of cause and effect is your best friend or your worst enemy depending on what you do with it. If you refuse to admit that your actions have results, you suffer consequences. If I exercise less, I end up in worse shape. If I'm casual about brushing my teeth, I get more cavities. If I watch TV instead of writing my book, I don't get to publish a book.

All our actions have effects. Those are the consequences. Fighting that principle is as silly as fighting gravity. Refusing to take ownership for our actions is like waking up each morning and being furious that gravity is still in play on our planet. "Ugh! I can't believe I can't leap fifty feet in the air with this cursed earthbound body. Stupid gravity! Maybe tomorrow will be different . . ."

If you embrace the law of cause and effect, however, you don't get consequences; you get compound interest. If I exercise more, I get in better shape. If I brush my teeth more, I have fewer cavities. If I write more, I publish more books. Those little actions I commit to again and again build up over time like compound interest. I might not see the effects quickly, but I'll definitely see them eventually. That's just how cause and effect works.

I looked at my finances and realized I had three options:

1. Ignore my money and live in the Comfort Zone as long as possible until a financial crisis kicked me out.
2. Declare that I'd become a financial expert, trying to do it all at once and running right into the Chaos Zone.
3. Turn money into an Easy Goal, a Middle Goal, and eventually a Guaranteed Goal that kept me in the Potential Zone.

I'd tried the first option for years, and to be honest with you, it worked pretty well. I'd ignore my money until there was a significant problem and then hustle my way out of it. The only problem was that I'd experienced how amazing life was in the

Potential Zone with other games in my life, and I wanted all five to be represented. I didn't want to be a bodybuilder who skipped leg day, bro, with my career, relationships, health, and fun goals working while my finances limped along.

I knew the second option wouldn't work long-term because the sprint approach had failed me too many times. Fool me once, shame on you. Fool me 783 times, shame on me!

Which left me with the third option. It was easy to pick that one because, much like looking back instead of forward to build my Best Moments List, I didn't have any other choice.

The biggest opportunity for dealing with my money was in the realm of my company. My personal finances were fine because my wife Jenny is involved. My company's finances, on the other hand, were the Wild, Wild West since I was the only one really looking at them.

I wrote down "Manage the company's finances" as my goal but quickly realized that was too shapeless. You can't turn a goal that undefined into actions, so I started listing out some specific Easy Goals instead:

1. Find a copy of my company's monthly PNL (profit and loss).
2. Print that copy since I'm a paper guy.
3. Pack that copy on a business trip so I could review it in Houston.
4. Label a manila folder with "PNL" so I have a place to put next week's document too.
5. Tell my wife I am going to review the PNL.
6. Schedule a fifteen-minute review on my calendar.

7. Reschedule the fifteen-minute review on my calendar because I hate reviewing finances so much that I ghosted the first meeting with myself.

Do those things sound impressive? I hope not, because an Easy Goal isn't supposed to impress anyone. An Easy Goal should be something like, "Find your running shoes" or "Look up the hours for the gym" or "Buy trash bags for the decluttering project." When I say you should go easy at the beginning, I mean you should go really easy.

It took me about three weeks to accomplish those goals. Even though it was really only about an hour of work, I managed to spread it out over twenty-one days. When there's a goal I'm avoiding, I tend to continue avoiding it. And I'm not the only one who does that.

Chris Ruch, a creative director in Pennsylvania, told me he was "petrified/overwhelmed by the idea of filing." His approach was simple: throw all the papers in a box and hopefully never have to deal with them. Do you have that same box in your house right now? What about the drawer of tangled cords and chargers for every phone you've owned for the last ten years? I can see my own rat nest from where I am sitting. What inspired Chris to do a few Easy Goals with his paperwork? His mom had a near-death experience. "Having to hunt through her paperwork, I had a revelation that I should get my papers in order." Like most things we put off, it turned out to be easier than he thought. "It really wasn't hard after all," he said. "It just took a little time."

In chapter 5, I said that there are two reasons people leave their Comfort Zones: involuntary crisis and voluntary trick.

When Chris's mom almost died, he experienced an involuntary crisis that inspired him to get his own life in order.

Rebekah Phillips told me that she "dealt with a broken dishwasher soap dispenser for over a year before googling it, watching a two-minute YouTube video, and simply fixing it with very little effort." Dozens of people shared stories online with me just like this one, and the result was always the same: they were surprised at how easy it was to fix something that appeared insurmountable.

Chris's Easy Goals of dealing with his paperwork could turn into a Middle Goal—every new year comes with new paperwork that needs to be filed—but I doubt Rebekah's goal will grow bigger. She probably didn't decide to become an appliance repair technician after her soap dispenser fix. Not every Easy Goal turns into a Middle Goal, but some do, which is why I asked myself two questions after I finished my first few financial actions:

1. Is it worth turning this into a Middle Goal?

2. If it is, what did I learn that I need to take forward?

The answer to the first question was "yes." After only a week of effort, I could see that focusing on my finances would pay dividends. Money also wasn't as scary as I thought it'd be. In hindsight that's not surprising, since experts tell us, "Exposure therapy has been firmly established as the best way to take on fears and phobias."[2]

I wish the solution to beating a fear was avoiding the fear altogether, but that doesn't work. "The reason is what psychologists call 'desensitization,' in which repeated exposure to something repellent or frightening makes it seem ordinary, prosaic, and certainly not scary."[3] It's funny to think of money as being repellent, but it was for me until I turned it into an Easy Goal.

I also learned something else important—reviewing my PNL without taking notes was worthless. I could check a box that I had done it, but it didn't really accomplish anything. To level up, I'd need to take notes.

For my Middle Goal, I committed to reviewing my PNL every week for a month. I had to coordinate that with my bookkeeper, arranging for her to send me an updated version every Wednesday afternoon. I had to schedule it ahead of time so that it actually happened, and I had to actively write down observations.

For example, I noticed that in December 2021 my company made 80 percent more revenue from public speaking than we have in other years. Most corporations don't do events at the end of the year because of the holidays. But after so many events had been canceled due to COVID, companies added some year-end events. They wouldn't be doing that in 2022, though, so we'd need to find another source of revenue in December.

I worked on my Middle Goals for a month and then asked those same two questions again:

1. Is it worth turning this into a Guaranteed Goal?
2. If it is, what did I learn that I need to take forward?

Again, the answer to the first question was "yes."

When I reviewed my PNL, I couldn't help but come up with some new ideas. Some were small, like selling our Finish

Calendar earlier in the year (FinishCalendar.com). Some were big, like writing a new book proposal before October so that we had a shot at closing a book contract before the year ended. It felt like I'd been flying a plane for years without looking at the instrument panel. "Ohhh, this is why it's been so bumpy and everyone keeps throwing up in the back. The landing gear is down and one engine is on fire. I bet things would be a lot smoother if I addressed that."

I also learned that taking notes was helpful, but I had to do something with them. I could fill up a hundred notebooks with ideas about our PNL, but unless I shared them with the team and turned them into projects, nothing would change.

The Guaranteed Goal started to take shape. I would commit to reviewing the PNL for fifteen minutes every week *and* averaging three actions from the review. Why averaging? Because the Middle Goal taught me that some weeks I'd have one action and some weeks I'd have five actions. I'd have greater long-term success if I made it an average, not a rigid rule. If my initial goal was to manage the company's finances, then I was guaranteed to succeed because at the end of the year I would've reviewed the PNL 52 times and taken 156 actions. It's impossible not to have a better set of finances if you touch that information that many times.

Could I have gone from zero to a hundred miles an hour, deciding out of the blue that I was going to review my PNL every week for a solid year? Maybe. Could I have skipped the Easy and Middle Goals? Maybe. But I wouldn't have learned how important the notes were, and I wouldn't have known that I needed an average of three actions per week. If the first forty-seven years of my life are any indication, I would've quit by about week three, overwhelmed at an annual goal I'd sprinted into instead of grown into.

You can definitely jump and try to reach out for the Guaranteed Goal rung at the top of the ladder on day one. That's not impossible, and you might be able to pull yourself up like you're doing a chin-up, with just enough willpower, grit, and discipline to make it work. Or you can walk up the ladder, step by step, learning along the way and getting better at every level.

The step-by-step approach makes progress so much easier, especially when it's a need-to area and not a want-to area of life. At first it might feel slow or counterintuitive to the overnight success culture we all wish were true, but the benefits of intentionally climbing the goal ladder always outweigh the cost.

What We're All Missing

One afternoon on a flight back to Nashville, I sat next to a thirty-one-year-old pharmaceutical manager. This was unusual because it was a Thursday flight, which usually means the plane is packed with bachelorette parties headed to Music City for a honky-tonk weekend. In the aviation industry this is what's known as a "woo-hoo flight" because that's what the bride-to-be yells the entire way.

The young man sitting next to me told me his story. He'd progressed quickly through his company, smashing each level of performance until he'd plateaued in his current position. The only other job available was his boss's, and he was way too young to be going anywhere soon.

The **BENEFITS** of intentionally

CLIMBING THE
GOAL LADDER

always outweigh the **COST**.

He could see the Comfort Zone calling, and he bristled when older neighbors told him, "You're already doing fine! I wasn't where you are at that age." He wanted something new, something more challenging, something bigger.

High performers are tempted in that moment to throw a grenade into their lives and change everything. Remember, "all or none" is what we often think are the only options for life change. Instead, I challenged him to turn an Easy Goal into a Middle Goal, and a Middle Goal eventually into a Guaranteed Goal.

All he had to do was find three career goals he was mildly interested in. "Go explore podcasts, mentorship, and leadership," I told him. Maybe he'd fall in love with a podcast he starts for young professionals who are also trying to prevent early plateaus. Maybe he'd find a mentor who could open his eyes to new opportunities at his current company. Maybe, since he'd only had his management position for six months, he could explore becoming a better leader.

Those are Easy Goals to try, and any one of them could be turned into a Middle Goal. If I met him six months later on another flight, maybe he would tell me he'd committed to recording a new podcast every week for three months or attending one new leadership event. Maybe a year later he would tell me his Guaranteed Goal. Perhaps reading about mentorship would have turned into finding a mentor, which would have turned into monthly meetings to review his progress. Another flight home could find him firmly in the Potential Zone, no longer concerned about getting stuck in the Comfort or Chaos Zones.

I hope that happens to him.

I hope that happens to you too.

If we were on a flight together, I'd tell you the exact same thing I told him: You're capable of more than you think. There's a path that's easy to follow. Anyone can do it.

I'd fit as much of this book into that trip as I could, but that's the problem with the flight from Atlanta to Nashville. It only takes thirty-nine minutes. There's only so much you can discuss. I didn't even get to tell that young man the most important thing about the Potential Zone that I'm about to tell you.

Entry is free, but you're going to need a scorecard to make sure you can stay.

17

Create a Scorecard to Know That You're Winning

Twitter was my first social media love.

Prior to becoming a dumpster fire of political fighting, click-baiting, and outrage, it was my favorite platform. Since I was a marketing copywriter, it instantly appealed to the part of me trained to write headlines. I was a soundbite machine and churned out more than 80,000 tweets over the years. Most of them were ridiculous observations about whatever was happening in my day and disappeared quickly. For example, "I once told an 18yo that I used to get Netflix delivered to me in the mail and I'm pretty sure he thought I was lying." A handful of my tweets caught traction, though, and stuck around.

One of my most popular is, "Don't compare your beginning to someone else's middle." That thought got turned into hundreds of Pinterest images, driftwood wall art, and even postcards in New Zealand. Someone mailed me the set, which included other equally impressive social media influencers like Gandhi and Eleanor Roosevelt. Finally, the contributions we three peers have been making to society are being recognized.

I think the tweet was so well received because it's true. You shouldn't compare your beginning to someone else's middle. You shouldn't compare your first book to Stephen King's thirtieth book, or your first business plan to Steve Jobs' iPhone launch, or your first push-up to The Rock's one millionth.

We all know that intellectually. No one believes comparison is a healthy activity, but how do we really stop doing it?

How do we break the stranglehold of comparison, something we've struggled with for years—keep up with the Joneses!—when social media makes it easier than ever to do? The most common advice usually does what I did in that tweet and just tells us to stop doing it.

"Quit it!"

"Take a break from social media!"

"Go on a digital detox!"

If that doesn't work, what if you tried gratitude instead?

"Be grateful!"

"Believe in yourself!"

"Count your blessings!"

Last but certainly not least is, "What if you encourage the person you're jealous of? Celebrate your enemy until they are no longer your enemy."

Those all seem like helpful solutions on the surface, but have you tried any of them? I have—for years. Did they work any better for you than they did for me? Or were they short-term fixes that didn't provide lasting change?

The reason none of those approaches work is that they all fail to answer the most important question: "Why do I compare myself to other people?"

The Answer

You don't have to go on a long, personal vision quest to figure out the answer to that question. I'll tell you right now.

The reason you compare yourself to others is that your brain wants to know you're making progress in life. Over time this desire might morph into a form of insecurity, materialism, or vanity, but at the root of comparison is your brain trying to answer the basic question "How are we doing?"

Can you blame it?

Have you ever had a friend who navigates for you in the passenger seat but doesn't give you the directions soon enough? He doesn't say, "In half a mile, you're going to take a right at the third light." Instead, as you get to an intersection, he blurts out, "Oh, this is your right—turn, turn, turn!" It's an annoying experience because you never really feel confident about where you're going or how the trip is progressing. Are we close to our final destination? Do we have a long way to go? Are we making good time?

Your brain wants to know that about your life, too, especially when it comes to the five big games of career, finances, relationships, health, and fun.

How are we doing in our career? Should we be further along by now? Are we in the right spot? Is it too late to jump to another profession? Have we made the most of our opportunities?

How are our relationships? Do we have enough friends? Does anybody really know us? Does everyone get lonely like this, or is it just us?

How are our finances? Are we supposed to have more money saved up by now? Is our 401(k) on track? Will we be able to pay for college? If there's a recession, will we survive it?

How is our health? Are we in shape? Are we out of shape? Are we getting enough sleep? Should we be putting collagen in our coffee or eating less gluten?

Are we having fun right now? Are you allowed to have fun as an adult, or is that something that only happens in your twenties? Have we lost our mojo? What is mojo? Am I too young to be this into bird-watching? Is this all there is to life, or is there something more?

Your brain is constantly curious about your progress, and so are you.

You wouldn't work hard on a diet and exercise plan for a year if you didn't get any progress updates. You'd get frustrated at your job if the boss never gave any feedback about your performance. You wouldn't go on vacation with someone who told you, "We're just going to the ocean. I can't tell you which one, how we're getting there, or where we'll be staying." You want information, and so does your brain.

But if you ask most people, "How are your relationships going? How's your health? How is your career?" they offer vague answers if they offer any. "It's good. It's fine. Day by day. Just putting one foot in front of the other."

That's not good enough for your brain. Vague answers don't satisfy the most curious part of your body. In the moment, your brain doesn't stop seeking a progress update on life. It just says, "Fine, if you won't tell me the score, I'll go look at someone else's scorecard and see if I can figure it out that way." That's how comparison always starts.

In the absence of a scorecard, your brain will use someone else's. That's a big problem because when you score your life against someone else's scorecard, you will always come up lacking. I make a terrible Brené Brown. I'm the worst James Clear. You'd be embarrassed at how bad I am at being Jim Collins.

Occasionally, I forget this and compare myself to a handful of other successful authors. I essentially score my life against theirs. When I do this, I completely forget that we're not playing the same game.

A single man, without any kids, building a speaking career while living in LA has very little in common with me. I've been married for twenty-two years. I'm raising two teenage daughters. I live in the suburbs of Nashville. We may share a career game, but our other four games are wildly different.

For example, fall is the busiest season for public speaking at corporate events, but I limit my Friday night commitments so I can be home for high school football games with my family. There's no other place I'd rather be than sitting in those rickety stands under the Friday Night Lights. But if I peek at my phone during halftime, I can quickly become envious that some other speaker is speaking at a big event in Colorado Springs at that moment. The entire football stadium disappears as I spin off into a bout of comparison.

Gratitude won't fix that.

Cheering for the other person won't stop that.

Taking a social media fast won't change that.

In the absence of a **SCORECARD,** your brain will use **SOMEONE ELSE'S.**

The only thing that will end your temptation to compare yourself to other people is when you finally have your own scorecard to look at.

How to Build Your Own Scorecard

As of this exact moment, I've spent 410.25 hours crafting ideas this year.

I exercised twenty-six times in the last thirty days. I've taken vitamins five times in the last week.

These aren't random activities for me but rather are specific signs that I'm living in the Potential Zone. The vitamins are an Easy Goal. The exercise is a Middle Goal. Crafting ideas is a Guaranteed Goal. They are three actions I've committed to tracking.

If you asked me whether I was living up to my potential, I wouldn't tell you, "I think so" or "I feel like I am." I'd tell you I've spent 410.25 hours crafting ideas this year. I exercised twenty-six times in the last thirty days. I've taken vitamins five times in the last week.

The only reason I know any of those facts is that I have scorecards. These days I don't have much time to compare myself to other people because my entire life is littered with scorecards.

My wall chart tracks my writing hours.

My notebook tracks my daily goals.

The mini whiteboard on my desk tracks my weekly tasks.

The Goodreads app tracks my reading progress.

The behavior chart tracks how many times I've been kind to my family.

The Delta app tracks how often I've flown this year and the progress I'm making toward better status. (Like a perpetual aviation bridesmaid, I'm always platinum, never diamond.)

The Wells Fargo app gives me updates on my finances.

Instagram, Twitter, and Facebook give me reams of information about the growth of my social media.

Buzzsprout informs me about my podcast downloads.

Apple tracks how many podcast reviews I have.

My calendar shows me how many meetings I'm committed to this week.

Strava tells me how many miles I've run this year.

Amazon gives me a ranking of my book sales.

My profit and loss sheet gives me a temperature check of my business.

My inbox tells me how my communication is going with colleagues, clients, and friends.

My bookshelf tells me how my Guaranteed Goal of writing a stack of books taller than me is progressing. That's a long-term goal I have. I'm up to about my waist right now, including foreign editions, thanks for asking.

I didn't even have to leave the chair I'm sitting in to see all of those. I bet I could find a dozen more scorecards in other parts of the house. Some of them I created, like the big wall chart I drew that shows how many hours I've spent on ideas. Some of them I just utilize, like the Strava exercise app. They're all different, but every one of the scorecards is beneficial to me.

If you've ever felt the aimlessness of the Comfort Zone or the behind feeling that accompanies the panicked rush of the Chaos Zone, the reason is the same—you don't have scorecards.

Fortunately, they are the easiest things in the world to find because a scorecard can be ANYTHING that measures progress for your goal.

I put ANYTHING in all caps because the first question people always ask me about scorecards is, "Does this count?" And the answer is yes. Anything can be a scorecard.

A scorecard can be ANYTHING that measures progress for your goal.

An empty laundry basket is a scorecard if the game you're playing is "deal with all the laundry."

The timer on your iPhone is a scorecard if you need to focus on a project for thirty minutes.

Seven boxes you scribble on a Post-it note and check off for a weekly goal is a scorecard.

A mindfulness app that shows how many times you've meditated this month is a scorecard.

Anything can be a scorecard, and there aren't a lot of rules for this particular tool. There are only two, actually:

1. Make it visual.

2. Use it.

That's it. You have to be able to see the progress and you have to engage with it. Once you do, you're going to discover that scorecards are the fastest, funnest, most inspiring way to know you're in the Potential Zone. And high performers always use them.

David Trautman has a scorecard for the books he reads. He's the CEO of Park National Bank. There are some people in life you wouldn't bet against. The minute you meet them, you know that regardless of what life throws at them, they are going to make it. David is one of those people. I would not bet against him.

When I spoke to his company, I asked him if he had a book recommendation for me. I'm always curious to figure out what people living in the Potential Zone are reading. Instead of suggesting a title or two, he emailed me a beautifully formatted PDF list of ninety-four books organized into five different categories. If you work for David, you can request any of the titles for free, ranging from *Green Eggs and Ham* in the selling category to *The Federalist Papers* in the personal development category.

David and his entire staff don't have to guess if he's invested in learning more each year. They can watch the list grow. It's a scorecard.

When I interviewed high-performing people, that was one of the few things they all had in common: their lives were full of scorecards. How did they build them? By answering three questions.

1. What am I going to measure?

The whole point of a scorecard is that we're tracking progress. Which part of the progress are you going to measure? The three most common items to measure are *time, actions,* and *results*. When I write down how many hours I spent writing each week, I'm measuring time. When I check off a box on a chart after taking my vitamins, I'm measuring an action. When I update the amount of weight I lifted during a CrossFit workout, I'm measuring results.

It wouldn't make sense for me to track how long swallowing vitamins takes. I'm very fast with water, so time isn't a factor. I'm also not increasing the amount of vitamins each week, so results aren't worth tracking. I score the action: Did I take vitamins—yes or no?

Wayne Beck and his wife decided to measure debt they paid off, which is a form of results. "We kept score on a wall chart that we colored in as we went. Each time we knocked out a target, we rewarded our own effort with something cool, like a weekend away."

If your goal doesn't easily lend itself to measurement, don't worry. You can measure absolutely anything. Therapists use feelings scorecards to measure how patients are feeling. Doctors have scorecards for pain. And Grace Hagerty measured how many pounds of stuff she got rid of at her house.

Wait . . . what?

That's right. She told me, "When I needed to purge things, I weighed them as they went out of the house. I kept a chart. I put my house on a diet. I rid the house of several hundred pounds." I don't know if Grace took a before-and-after photo with a happy, skinny house holding up an old pair of pants it used to wear, but she should have.

2. How long will I measure it?

You could measure the progress of your goal for as short as three minutes or as long as a year. Jana Cinnamon, a partner and chief operating officer at a CPA firm, uses songs as mini scorecards that inspire her. "Instead of overthinking an email response," she says, "I give myself the length of one song to get it done and hit Send before the song ends." Who knew music could be such a perfect scorecard? She makes her musical scorecards even bigger sometimes. "I have a playlist that I work out to until it ends." When the playlist is over, so is the workout. The playlist is the scorecard and tracks her progress.

Some of the goals I measure take me a month to focus on. For those I draw an Action Tracker. It's a simple, paper-based chart that helps you keep a visual focus on the actions you're building into your life. To build an Action Tracker, you need:

1. A piece of paper
2. A pen
3. A ruler

Once you have your supplies, the next step is to create a list of actions that will make it easier to finish your goal. The action can be anything, as long as it can be accomplished every day. You wouldn't put "Write a book" on your list. That's not an action. That's a big goal. You would instead write, "Spend thirty minutes working on my new book." That's an action. You can track that.

Here are some actions I've tracked in my own life:

1. Making my bed every morning
2. Encouraging one person every day
3. Brushing and flossing three times a day
4. Reading ten pages a day
5. Drinking 64 ounces of water a day

You'll notice that those actions are all over the place. That's what's fun about an Action Tracker—you can apply it to any goal in your life.

Action Trackers work better for Middle Goals because Easy Goals have a much shorter time frame than thirty days. You can also break a Guaranteed Goal into thirty-day blocks. For example, I could take my Guaranteed Goal of eight hundred hours of ideas and measure it monthly.

Once you have your list, turn to the back of the book where I've included a sample Action Tracker for you so it's easy to use. On the left side, list all your actions. Along the top of the chart, fill in the days of the month.

Throughout the month, as you do the action each day, color in the box. The "T" on the last line is for "Total." I'm always curious at the end of the month to see how many days I accomplished my actions.

It's fun to start an Action Tracker on the first day of the month, but if today is the fifteenth, don't wait. You can start a thirty-day Action Tracker any day of the year.

Some goals are not measured by time-based metrics like weeks or months but rather by completion. If your goal is to lose a certain amount of weight, move cross-country, or pay off debt, you probably can't predict exactly when it will be done. So your measurement would focus on moving from start to finish, not day 1 to day 30.

3. Where will I measure it?

Hopefully by now you're starting to see that there's no "right" answer to these questions, there's only a "you" answer. It's your scorecard so it should fit your life.

When I posted a photo of my hand-drawn Action Tracker on Instagram one day, a woman named Niki Richardson commented, "That looks absolutely oppressive and awful." She wasn't mistaken; she just left out two important words: "for me." That's what she meant. "That looks absolutely oppressive and awful *for me.*"

The problem with self-help is that the author often leaves off those two key words. An extrovert writes a book about networking and then is surprised why so many introverts balk at her suggestions. A naturally organized person says the only way to be successful is to color-code each activity you do every day and then wonders why free-form, artistic people are hesitant. An early morning person gets up at 4 a.m. and then turns their personal passion into a prescription that everyone must do.

If you're going to tap into your potential, you must filter any advice you receive through your personality, strengths, desires, and life.

I'm not a naturally detailed person. I struggle with staying organized, so doing a thirty-day Action Tracker each month helps me stay in the Potential Zone. Maybe you're just the opposite. That's great—figure out a different execution that works for you.

Michelle Connors made a board game type of challenge like Candyland to track one of her goals. Another time she used an image of a football field, and every ten yards was a goal. She also created a map to use for her steps goal. A different time she did a Tetris-style board. I don't know if any of those would work for me, but they worked for Michelle, and that's perfect.

Jake Puhl, the CEO of Dentist Entrepreneur Organization, uses Notion, a planning software app, to build all of his scorecards. I'm a paper person and tend to get lost if I build my scorecards digitally, but he loves it.

Adam Savage, cohost of the show *MythBusters*, devotes two whole chapters of his delightful book *Every Tool's a Hammer* to the lists and checkboxes he uses as scorecards in his work. He knows that "you can't count on external sources of motivation to be there when you've hit a wall with a project, or you're in the dead days halfway through. You will need to create your own motivation to keep going, and the momentum that springs from a checklist that is more filled in than not can be just the thing to fuel your fire."[1]

It doesn't matter whether you use a Spotify playlist to track how long you focus on a workout, a software program to measure how you're building a small business, or a list to build momentum for Star Wars props like Adam did in his time at Industrial Light & Magic. What matters is that you have a visible scorecard and that you use it.

You also don't need to be crafty, creative, or organized to create a scorecard. Some of mine are so easy even a kindergartner could figure them out. The chart I'm using to be kind to my family 365 times this year is actually designed for six-year-olds. I bought it on Amazon. It's a huge poster of a traffic light covered in a grid of small boxes. I think it's meant to reward little Timmy for not biting in class or young Alissa for not drinking Elmer's glue when the teacher isn't looking. Instead, every time I do something kind for my wife or kids, I put a green smile sticker in one of the boxes.

I know that's ridiculous, but I was encouraged to try this by author Marshall Goldsmith. In his book *The Earned Life*, he shares, "A friend once mocked me for tracking how many times I said something nice to my wife each day. 'You shouldn't have to be reminded to be nice to your wife,' he said." To which Goldsmith responded, "Evidently, I do." He goes on to say, "I'm not ashamed that I need a reminder to behave better. It would be shameful if I knew it and didn't do anything about it."[2]

That's the beauty of a scorecard. It gives you a visual, practical method to do something about it. And the "it" can be anything.

A good example of an "it" you've probably never noticed is at Costco. Fifteen feet up on the wall at the front of the store is a dry erase scorecard for all the cashiers. It measures three different categories: (1) items scanned per minute, (2) members processed per hour, and (3) top scanning. They update it every week, but they could probably just write "Tim R." in permanent marker because he refuses to lose.

I've never seen Tim at the store in Brentwood, Tennessee, but he is dominating that location. He currently scans 23.54 items per minute and processes 57.58 members per hour. It doesn't matter if you're buying a kayak, 144 batteries, and a pallet of dried squid snacks, you're spending about 80 seconds in Tim's line. Whenever I'm in the store, I ask the other cashiers about him. "Oh yeah, Tim," they say with begrudging admiration. "He's fast."

Having a visible, reward-based scorecard on the wall keeps the cashiers motivated. It also inspires creativity. On Reddit boards for Costco employees, cashiers post tips like this:

- While I give away the receipt and membership [card] with one hand, with the other I'm grabbing the next membership [card] and scanning it.

- Try to pass items from one hand to the other. Don't grab with both hands unless you must, and try not to twist your torso.
- Start memorizing where the bar codes are on each item for faster scanning.[3]

"Try not to twist your torso." Is that the most specific advice you've ever heard? It is, but it works. Costco makes an estimated $447 million in revenue per day.[4] Per day! I make slightly less than that myself, but if a scorecard can help Costco make $163 billion every year, could adding a few scorecards improve my performance too?

I think so. I've just got to remember not to twist my torso.

The Biggest Unexpected Benefit of a Scorecard

Comparing yourself to other people is the form of comparison that gets all the attention, but it's not the one that causes the most damage in our pursuit of potential. There's actually an even worse source of comparison that trips people up. The crazy thing is we never see it coming. Do you know who you really compare yourself to?

Yourself.

It's tempting to compare your current life to your old life or your imagined life and come up short. I didn't realize this was such an issue until I dug into the research for this book.

A participant named Valerie asked me, "How do I continue to move forward on goals with an aging parent with dementia who requires five to ten hours a week and an adult daughter in the hospital with kidney failure?"

Katie said, "I have a toddler and don't use daycare. My husband works ridiculous hours at an intense job, and I am a fairly new business owner. How do you prioritize it all?"

Holly said, "I haven't been able to get my business to the level I desire, and I recently became a widow and solo parent."

Reginald asked, "How do I stop beating myself up and still hit my real estate goals while caring for my mom alone at home, who is diagnosed with advanced dementia?"

My answer to each of those difficult situations was the same: *Create a new scorecard.*

Valerie was scoring herself against the old Valerie who hadn't been taking care of an aging parent or a daughter with kidney failure.

Katie was scoring herself against the old Katie who wasn't a toddler mom *and* a business owner.

Holly was scoring herself against the old Holly who wasn't a widow and a solo parent.

Reginald was scoring himself against the old Reginald who wasn't caring for a mom with advanced dementia.

When life changes, you need a new scorecard. Whether it's something positive like having a baby or starting a business, or something negative like a health crisis, if you don't change your scorecard, you'll waste precious time beating yourself up for expectations of performance that are no longer accurate.

I'm personally reminded of this principle every summer. I work from home and usually spend the first two weeks of June frustrated that I'm failing to get as much done as I did in May. What's the incredibly obvious reason for that? My kids are home. The neighborhood pool is open. It's summer! My quiet house is now an epicenter of activity. I've experienced this exact same thing for nine years in a row but always forget to adjust my expectations.

To be honest, initially I didn't think a scorecard would address that specific challenge. I was just experimenting with them because I wanted to track my goals. But when I started teaching others how to build scorecards, I'd watch relief wash over them.

I told Valerie, "Subtract those five to ten weekly hours that it takes to care for your mom from your expectations for your goals."

I cheered with Katie. "You own a new business, congratulations! Fold that into your other commitments and tweak everything."

I reminded Holly, "This is the first time you've ever been a widow and a solo parent. Increase the amount of grace you're giving yourself by about 100×."

I asked Reginald, "How long does it take to care for your mom? Adjust your real estate goals accordingly, at least for a season."

The words were different, but the heart of the advice was always the same: When you go through change, change your scorecard. Build a new one.

When you go through change, change your scorecard.

Is there anyone reading this book who hasn't experienced tremendous change in the last few years? Everyone needs a new scorecard after a pandemic. Everyone is comparing their current life to their pre-pandemic life on some level. And when you do that, not only do you end up beating yourself up, but you miss how amazing your new life can be going forward.

A Scorecard Is the Only Way to Know You're in the Potential Zone

We know scorecards work for kids, but for some reason we think adults don't need them. When I asked hundreds of people if they'd ever used scorecards for their goals, Rebecca Williams summed up the most typical response: "With the kids, yeah . . . but haven't thought about doing it with myself." From chore charts to reading lessons to potty training, we scorecard every part of childhood, but then at age eighteen we decide we no longer need them because life is easy now.

Has that been your experience with adulthood? Is it easier than childhood? Or is there a chance we need scorecards more than ever?

I need them.

You do too.

At the end of the day, the end of the week, the end of the year, or even the end of your life, I want you to have a really easy answer to the question, "Did I live up to my potential?"

"Yes, I did," you'll say, pointing to the fun scorecards you relied on to stay motivated during your Easy, Middle, and Guaranteed Goals. "There's the proof."

CONCLUSION

Go Back Down the Goal Ladder

Twenty-eight years after my disastrous freshman year at Samford University, I moved my oldest daughter L.E. into that same college. A few weeks after that, I was the keynote speaker at Samford's Family Weekend.

I was now a notable alumnus being honored as an example of what a graduate could accomplish. I had to smile before I took the stage because there wasn't a single person who thought that would ever happen when I was making shaved ice on the sidewalk in front of Walmart and getting put on social suspension by the dean of students. But that's the funny thing about potential.

It's never gone.

It's always waiting.

It's always available.

It's always willing to be redeemed at a moment's notice.

When you're ready to claim yours—and I think you are right now—I'll give you one last bit of encouragement: read this book in reverse.

No one dreams about Easy Goals.

No one says, "I want to walk a quarter mile! I want to write a hundred words! I want to declutter one drawer in my kitchen! I want to learn the G chord on guitar! I want to understand ten Italian words!"

We all dream much bigger than that about our potential, and we should.

I want to run a marathon!

I want to write a novel!

I want to declutter my entire house!

I want to master the guitar!

I want to move to Italy!

We have massive goals that we know take small steps, but how do we translate big dreams into micro actions? That's the gap where most people give up. Most people find it impossible to break a huge hope into daily deeds. Most people find it difficult to turn potential into a goal. But we're not most people. We're going to accomplish that by going back down the goal ladder we just climbed up in the previous chapters.

Review your Best Moments List. Remember when you got out your highlighter and identified the brightest parts of your life? What do you want more of? Do accomplishments, experiences, relationships, or objects light you up? The past is a gift that will inform your present and prepare your future.

Once you've got a rough sense of that, pick one of the five big games: career, finances, relationships, health, or fun. It can be anything! There are more than one hundred examples in this book alone.

Once you've got a game in mind, all you have to do is turn it into a Guaranteed Goal. Make sure your Guaranteed Goal

1. Has an extended time frame (ninety days to one year)
2. Is 100 percent in your control
3. Is easy to measure
4. Encourages you to be deliberate with your schedule (eight hours of work a week)
5. Sounds impossible when you tell people

If you can train for four months for a marathon, if you're in control of the training sessions, if you've got a scorecard to measure the miles, if you can clear your schedule for eight hours a week, and if friends think it's impossible, you're on the right track.

Then take your Guaranteed Goal and make it more manageable by shrinking it into a Middle Goal. Make sure your Middle Goal

1. Has a reasonable time frame (thirty to ninety days)
2. Is flexible
3. Doesn't fall apart if you miss a day
4. Encourages you to adjust your schedule (five hours of work a week)
5. Has patience built in

If you can commit to the first four weeks of running, if you're able to do a little bit every day, even just a slow walk around the block, if you're willing to forgive yourself if you miss a day, if you can find time without changing your schedule dramatically, and if you can make patient progress, you're in a good place.

Once you've got a game in mind, all you have to do is turn it into a **GUARANTEED GOAL.**

Finally, take your Middle Goal and make it even smaller by turning it into an Easy Goal. Make sure your Easy Goal

1. Has a short time frame (one to seven days)
2. Has obvious first steps
3. Is not expensive
4. Matches your current schedule (two hours of work a week)
5. Is so small it feels like "not enough"

If you can run two times this week, if you know how to find a good training plan, if you don't need to sign up for any expensive races yet, if you can easily fit it into your schedule, and if no one is impressed when you share your plans, you've got a perfect Easy Goal.

When you go back down the goal ladder, you've just accomplished what 99 percent of people fail to do.

You've taken a big game and made it actionable.

You took "someday" and translated it into "today."

You got around the Vision Wall.

You thwarted your stuck self.

You escaped the Comfort Zone, avoided the Chaos Zone, and took your first step into the Potential Zone.

You're no longer part of the 50 percent of people who feel they're leaving 50 percent of their potential untapped.

You're opening all your Christmas presents, not just half.

And I, for one, can't wait to see what you do with them.

ACTION TRACKER

MONTH: _____

ACTIONS	1	2	3	4	5	6	7	8	9	10	11	12	13	14	15	16	17	18	19	20	21	22	23	24	25	26	27	28	29	30	31	T

ACKNOWLEDGMENTS

I'd put "writing this book" on my Best Moments List, and the reason why is that I got to work with so many amazing people.

Jenny, I laugh every time I think about your favorite question to ask me when you read my manuscripts: "Jon, do you want feedback . . . or compliments?" Thanks for giving me both these last twenty-two years. You're on every page of this book. L.E. and McRae, I think it's time for us to write another book together because the last one was just too fun. I love you!

Ashley Holland, I can't believe we've already worked for seven years together. There's not a book, speech, course, podcast, or meeting that would ever happen without you! Giancarlo Lemmi, there are more than fifty real stories from real people in this book, and that's all because you chased them down. Thanks for your fantastic contribution.

Huge thank-you to the entire Baker team. I am thrilled that we get to do four more of these together. I've said it before and I'll say it again, "We are just getting started!" Brian Vos, thank you for shepherding this project from start to finish. I couldn't ask for a more insightful, patient, brilliant editor. Mark Rice, a book without a marketing wizard never gets read. Thanks for championing this book across every platform, medium, and shelf. Amy Nemecek, you magnify the humor, amplify the clarity, and serve the reader with every edit you offer. Laura Powell, thank you for turning my words into art with your creative designs. William Overbeeke, thanks for making the interior of the book as stunning as the exterior. Rachel O'Connor, thank you for flawlessly handling the millions of details that come with the acquisition of a new book.

Dwight Baker, Eileen Hanson, Holly Scheevel, Carson Kunnen, Olivia Peitsch, William Overbeeke, Nathan Henrion, and the entire Baker sales and marketing team. Thank you for bringing decades of excellence to every single decision we make together.

Mike Salisbury and Curtis Yates, thanks for challenging me each step of the way to make this book the best it could possibly be.

Mike Peasley, PhD, your research always takes a fun idea and adds jet fuel to it. Thanks for lending me your wisdom.

Caleb Peavy, Jessica Peavy, Katie Pilson, Amy Fenton, MC Tanksley, and Aaron Hovivian, thanks for turning my one-man show into a company that gets to change the world every single day.

And last but never least, thank you, the reader, for checking out my book. Without you, I'm just a guy in Nashville who writes awfully long diaries.

NOTES

Introduction

1. Simon Sinek, "How Great Leaders Inspire Action," TEDX Puget Sound, September 2009, https://www.ted.com/talks/simon_sinek_how_great_leaders _inspire_action?language=en.

Chapter 1 Go Back to the Future

1. John Tierney and Roy F. Baumeister, *The Power of Bad: How the Negativity Effect Rules Us and How We Can Rule It* (New York: Penguin Books, 2021), 71.

2. Martin E. P. Seligman, *Authentic Happiness: Using the New Positive Psychology to Realize Your Potential for Lasting Fulfillment* (New York: Free Press, 2002), 6.

Chapter 2 Build Your Best Moments List

1. Rita Elmkvist Nilsen, "How Your Brain Experiences Time," Norwegian University of Science and Technology, https://www.ntnu.edu/how-your-brain -experiences-time.

2. The comments from individuals that I share throughout the book are from private groups on Facebook and LinkedIn and are used with the generous permission of the named participants.

3. Elizabeth Dunn and Michael Norton, *Happy Money: The Science of Happier Spending* (New York: Simon & Schuster, 2013), 117.

Chapter 4 Trick the Hardest Person to Change

1. Daniel Z. Lieberman and Michael E. Long, *The Molecule of More: How a Single Chemical in Your Brain Drives Love, Sex, and Creativity—and Will Determine the Fate of the Human Race* (Dallas: BenBella Books, 2018), 201.

2. Mihaly Csikszentmihalyi, *Finding Flow: The Psychology of Engagement with Everyday Life* (New York: Basic Books, 1997), 59.

3. Csikszentmihalyi, *Finding Flow*, 59.

4. Csikszentmihalyi, *Finding Flow*, 59.
5. Lieberman and Long, *The Molecule of More*, 5.
6. Lieberman and Long, *The Molecule of More*, 6.

Chapter 6 Pick the Big Game You Want to Win

1. Marshall Goldsmith, *What Got You Here Won't Get You There: How Successful People Become Even More Successful* (New York: Hachette, 2007), 180.
2. Goldsmith, *What Got You Here*, 180.
3. Gay Hendricks, *The Big Leap: Conquer Your Hidden Fear and Take Life to the Next Level* (San Francisco: HarperOne, 2010).

Chapter 7 Escape the Comfort Zone with an Easy Goal

1. Jeffery J. Downs and Jami L. Downs, *Streaking: The Simple Practice of Conscious, Consistent Actions That Create Life-Changing Results* (n.p.: Page Two Books, 2020), 38.

Chapter 8 Skip the Chaos Zone with a Middle Goal

1. Quoted in Morgan Housel, *The Psychology of Money: Timeless Lessons on Wealth, Greed, and Happiness* (Petersfield, UK: Harriman House, 2020), 142.

Chapter 9 Plan a Calendar Heist

1. Oliver Burkeman, *Four Thousand Weeks: Time Management for Mortals* (New York: Farrar, Straus and Giroux, 2021), 95.
2. Jon Acuff (@JonAcuff), Twitter, June 1, 2022, 2:50 p.m., https://twitter.com/JonAcuff/status/1532072076198088704.

Chapter 10 Find Your Favorite Fuel

1. Bryan K. Smith, "What Kind of Fuel Do Rockets Use and How Does It Give Them Enough Power to Get into Space?," *Scientific American*, February 13, 2006, https://www.scientificamerican.com/article/what-kind-of-fuel-do-rock/.
2. Smith, "What Kind of Fuel Do Rockets Use?"
3. Warren Buffett, pledge letter, The Giving Pledge, accessed October 25, 2022, https://givingpledge.org/pledger?pledgerId=177.

Chapter 11 Achieve the Best Kind of Accomplishment

1. "Reinvent Your Life, Raise Millions of Dollars, Do Work That Matters: The Scott Harrison Story," *All It Takes Is a Goal* (podcast), episode 71, May 2, 2022, https://podcasts.apple.com/us/podcast/atg-71-reinvent-your-life-raise-millions-of-dollars/id1547078080?i=1000559295402.

Chapter 12 Get Crafty without Any Glitter

1. Brendan Leonard, *I Hate Running and You Can Too: How to Get Started, Keep Going, and Make Sense of an Irrational Passion* (New York: Artisan Books, 2021), 56.

2. Mihaly Csikszentmihalyi, *Finding Flow: The Psychology of Engagement with Everyday Life* (New York: Basic Books, 1997), 105.

3. Csikszentmihalyi, *Finding Flow*, 105.

4. Csikszentmihalyi, *Finding Flow*, 105–6.

Chapter 13 Find Your People, Find Your Potential

1. Paul Graham, "The Refragmentation," paulgraham.com, January 2016, http://paulgraham.com/re.html.

2. Peter F. Drucker, "Managing Knowledge Means Managing Oneself," *Leader to Leader* no. 16 (Spring 2000), http://rlaexp.com/studio/biz/conceptual _resources/authors/peter_drucker/mkmmo_org.pdf.

Chapter 15 Guarantee Your Success

1. Quoted in Madsen Pirie, "Death and Taxes," Adam Smith Institute, November 13, 2019, https://www.adamsmith.org/blog/death-and-taxes.

Chapter 16 Turn Fears into Goals and Watch Them Fall

1. "Next Time, What Say We Boil a Consultant," *Fast Company*, October 31, 1995, https://www.fastcompany.com/26455/next-time-what-say-we-boil -consultant.

2. Joscha Böhnlein et al., "Factors Influencing the Success of Exposure Therapy for Specific Phobia: A Systematic Review," *Neuroscience and Biobehavioral Reviews* 108 (January 2020): 796–820, https://doi.org/10.1016/j.neubiorev.2019 .12.009.

3. Arthur C. Brooks, *From Strength to Strength: Finding Success, Happiness, and Deep Purpose in the Second Half of Life* (New York: Portfolio, 2022), 105.

Chapter 17 Create a Scorecard to Know That You're Winning

1. Adam Savage, *Every Tool's a Hammer: Life Is What You Make It* (New York: Atria Books, 2020), 58.

2. Marshall Goldsmith and Mark Reiter, *The Earned Life: Lose Regret, Choose Fulfillment* (New York: Currency, 2022), 141.

3. juancho0808, "[Employee] Cashier statistics question," Reddit, 2018, https:// www.reddit.com/r/Costco/comments/a4wvgr/employee_cashier_statistics _question/.

4. Marques Thomas, "How Much Does Costco Make a Second, Minute, Hour, Day, and Month?" Query Sprout, May 12, 2021, https://querysprout .com/how-much-does-costco-make-a-second-minute-hour-day-and-month/.

JON ACUFF is the *New York Times* bestselling author of nine books, including *Soundtracks: The Surprising Solution to Overthinking*, *Your New Playlist: The Student's Guide to Tapping into the Superpower of Mindset*, and the *Wall Street Journal* #1 bestseller *Finish: Give Yourself the Gift of Done*. When he's not writing or recording his popular podcast, *All It Takes Is a Goal*, Acuff can be found on a stage as one of INC's Top 100 Leadership Speakers. He's spoken to hundreds of thousands of people at conferences, colleges, and companies around the world, including FedEx, Range Rover, Microsoft, Nokia, and Comedy Central. Known for his insights wrapped in humor, Acuff's fresh perspective on life has given him the opportunity to write for *Fast Company*, *Harvard Business Review*, and *Time* magazine. Jon lives outside of Nashville, Tennessee, with his wife, Jenny, and two daughters. To learn more, visit JonAcuff.com

@JonAcuff | **@AuthorJonAcuff**

5 IDEAS TO SHOUT ABOUT!

Every Friday I send out an action-packed, often hilarious collection of pure awesome! These are the kinds of ideas that if you came to my house for dinner, my wife, Jenny, would end up saying, "Jon, you're shouting about those ideas. Take it down a notch."

The ideas include the following:

1. Book recommendations

2. Songs you haven't heard but will undoubtedly love

3. Links to fresh videos

4. Things I think are funny

5. Tips on the little corners of life I know a little about (writing, speaking, entrepreneurship, parenting, Yanni, etc.)

And a whole lot more.

Don't miss a single issue. Sign up for free today!

Visit JonAcuff.com/Newsletter

CONNECT WITH JON ONLINE!

@JonAcuff

@AuthorJonAcuff

To learn more, visit JonAcuff.com

To see him live or to schedule Jon Acuff for your next event, visit BookJonAcuff.com

"It would be impossible for me to give Jon a higher level of endorsement. Over the past ten years Jon has presented to our groups on seven occasions and has been our highest-rated presenter each time. I have zero hesitation in giving you my highest level of assurances that Jon will have an incredible impact on your event."
—Ron Kitchens, Southwest Michigan First

"We would bring Jon Acuff back to Walmart anytime. He not only has executive presence, but he has lived the role and responsibilities. His ability to talk to any level is incredible. He is professional, honest, and human. He inspired our team and made the difference."
—Clara Park, Walmart International Support Team

"Akamai's marketing and sales leadership teams are still buzzing about Jon's talks. It's a testament to not only his obvious talent with humor and impactful storytelling in front of a crowd, but how he was willing to listen and adapt the content to what the teams needed to hear."
—Ari Weil, VP Product Marketing, Akamai

Jon is one of INC's Top 100 Leadership Speakers. He's spoken to hundreds of thousands of people at conferences, colleges, and companies around the world, including FedEx, Nissan, Microsoft, Lockheed Martin, Chick-fil-A, Nokia, and Comedy Central. Known for his insights wrapped in humor, Jon always provides a mix of inspiration and instruction that leaves audiences ready to turn their ideas into actions.

ALL IT TAKES IS A GOAL PODCAST

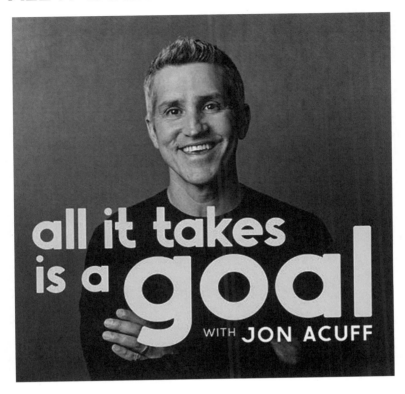

Each week, join Jon and guests to explore the best tips, tricks, and techniques to get from where you are today to where you want to be tomorrow. The future belongs to finishers, and this podcast is going to teach you how to be one. All it takes is a goal.

Listen and subscribe at **AllItTakesIsAGoal.com**